Lilly and Dennis Klepp have demonstrated what is ~~possible~~ when their hearts are a new life in serving Jesus Christ in one of the most difficult parts of the world—South Sudan—a country I have visited and worked in for many years.

This story will give you a firsthand look into what motivated a young couple to leave their life of ease behind and go to the ends of the earth for the sake of the gospel. The Klepps' story will touch your heart, and I hope motivate you to pray for them as they continue this remarkable ministry in Africa.

Franklin Graham
President and CEO
Samaritan's Purse

This is an amazing story of obedience, surrender, and sacrifice well beyond the average life. It's also a story of passion, power, and purpose. Lilly and Dennis Klepp have fully invested themselves in the orphans of war-torn South Sudan. They have established orphanages, schools, and healthcare centers, but it is their visible love and compassion for people in need that is touching and changing lives. They are the real deal, and I am honored to know them. Read and be inspired!

Terry Meeuwsen
Director, Orphan's Promise
Cohost, *The 700 Club*

In 1999 Lillian Ann Klepp heard a story that would change her life—a presentation about civil war, genocide, slavery, and lost children in Sudan. In those moments God's call began to reveal itself, and the prayerful journey that followed would prove the incredible strength of His love in the darkest of places.

Adventures Under the Mango Tree is a remarkable account of the compelling "burden for Sudan" that inspired Lillian and her husband, Dennis, to leave their home in Wisconsin and move across the world to war-torn Yei, Sudan, where they founded the ministry Harvesters Reaching the Nations. Over the past decade Harvesters has become a refuge of hope and care in South Sudan, with two orphanages and schools serving hundreds of children.

The need is great for ministry and aid in Sudan. Decades of conflict between Sudan and South Sudan have left deep scars and lingering rivalries. Fear pervades villages, and brutal attacks continue against innocent lives. We can rejoice in knowing that the news of Christ's eternal peace is spreading because of messengers like Lillian, now affectionately known as "Mama Lilly." Through her story we see the extraordinary power of God to enable His servants to do good in the world. We see the mighty role of prayer in dealing with any obstacle—from the uncertain fate of a malnourished child to battles with cancer and malaria. We see the bridging of cultural differences and the challenges of living in a place so different from home.

In this story Mama Lilly writes that on her first visit to Sudan in a room full of men armed with AK-47s an official told her, "Preach the light to my people." Indeed, for more than thirteen years she has done just that, sharing with compassion and grace the glory of God to those in desperate need of deliverance.

The Honorable Roger F. Wicker
U.S. Senator, Mississippi

Adventures Under the Mango Tree turns casual Christianity upside down. Like reading the personal journal of Mama Lilly, the reader will quickly awaken to the truth that you cannot love God without obedience. This book is about a faithful God who loves and calls people to be His church and sends them out to advance the kingdom in the most unlikely places. For Mama Lilly and Dennis, God's call took them from a rural community in Wisconsin to the war-torn nation of South Sudan to preach the good news and to rescue and raise up God's children. Come follow Jesus into this supernatural journey of life under the mango tree.

Senior Pastor Todd Gaston
Mount Ararat Baptist Church
Stafford, Virginia

Adventures Under the Mango Tree

Adventures Under the Mango Tree

A Story of Hope in War-Torn Sudan

LILLIAN ANN KLEPP
"Mama Lilly"

BEDFORD, TEXAS

Published in association with Creative Enterprises Studio, PO Box 224, Bedford, Texas 76022. CreativeEnterprisesStudio.com

ISBN: 978-0-9890521-7-7

Library of Congress Control Number: 2013945103

Cover Design: It's Just a Pixel. Itsjustapixel.com
Interior Design: Inside Out Design & Typesetting

Printed in the United States of America
14 15 16 17 18 19 20   MG   7 6 5 4 3 2

To the voiceless orphans
of South Sudan

All proceeds from this book support the work
of Harvesters in South Sudan

CONTENTS

Contents

Acknowledgments

This story would not have been possible without my wonderful husband, Dennis, who has worked so much behind the scenes.

We are forever indebted to our friends, Bishop Elias and Anngrace Taban, who are from Yei. They have been such an encouragement and help to Dennis and me during all these years we have been in Sudan. They have a real heart for the Lord and for helping their people. They have made many sacrifices to help their country. I pray God will continue to bless them both as they serve Him.

Finally, we are grateful for the many members of the body of Christ and the churches who have believed in our vision and faithfully supported us. We couldn't have done this without them.

Introduction

$\mathcal{B}$ack in 2001, during the height of Sudan's civil war, an ordinary couple from Wisconsin stepped out in faith to respond to the largely unheard voices of thousands of Sudanese children whose lives had been devastated by the seemingly endless conflict ravaging their country.

Dennis, a construction company owner, and his wife, Lillian, a physical therapist assistant and worship leader, are two people who had previously been living an ordinary life. Then they decided to do the extraordinary—sell all their possessions and go to a foreign land to be the hands and feet of Jesus to the less fortunate.

Adventures Under the Mango Tree is the real life story of what God can do when His children submit to His call and choose to live as "living sacrifices" (Romans 12:1–2). As you embark on this journey alongside Lillian, "Mama Lilly" as she is affectionately known, you will encounter the humorous and heart wrenching, the tragic and miraculous. You will also discover God's heart for the less fortunate (James 1:27) and His love for the people of Sudan.

You will be amazed to see that what began as a ninety-nine-acre landscape full of mango trees has been transformed into two orphanages on two different campuses that provide for the daily needs (both physical and spiritual) of nearly two hundred children. You will learn about Harvesters' school, which provides education for more than five hundred local children, and as of 2012, a recently opened hospital, His House of Hope, that has become a beacon of hope amidst the overwhelming medical needs of women and children in a place described as among the worst in the world.

So join "Mama Lilly" on her journey to Sudan. Meet the people and places that have forever changed her life and, most importantly, learn more about our great God and His power to change lives and bring hope to one of the most remote regions of the world.

Where in the World Is Sudan?

AFRICA

Sudan
Pre - Independence Day

Post - Independence Day
July 9, 2011

SUDAN

SOUTH
SUDAN

South Sudan, Africa

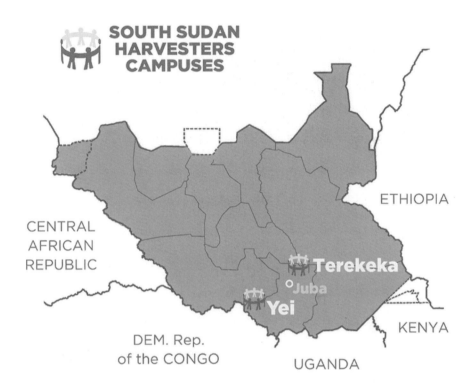

ONE

Beginnings
(1954–1980)

$\mathcal{I}$ grew up in both Milwaukee and Waukesha, Wisconsin, with my older brother, Martin. Our father was a truck driver and was home only on weekends. Our mother was a factory worker. As we grew up both our parents were wonderful people, but my father struggled hard when he drank. Every weekend he would go out drinking, come back to the house, and beat our mother. I remember screaming and crying, begging him to stop hitting her. Most weekends I would stay home because I was too afraid to leave Mother alone. Before long I assumed the role of caretaker in my family.

When I got to seventh grade at the age thirteen, I began to drink and get into trouble. By eighth grade it became too difficult to concentrate on school, so I decided to quit. At seventeen I reconnected with a guy named Dennis who I had known since I was little. He had just returned home from serving in Vietnam. As we started dating he and I became so smitten with each other that we decided to get married.

In 1972, right after I turned eighteen, Dennis and I married. Because Dennis was not the legal age of twenty-one at the time, his folks had to sign permission for us to be married. By 1973 we welcomed our first son, Corey. Four years later we celebrated our second son, Lance. At the time I had no idea what was in

Dennis and Lilly Klepp
October 21, 1972

store for us when it came to raising our family, but looking back I can see the Lord was at work in my soul.

Over the next several years, Dennis' mother became a Christian, and the Lord continued to bring people into our lives to share the gospel with us. At that time we felt led to be closer to his parents, so we moved to northern Wisconsin.

By 1980 both Dennis and I had given our hearts to Christ and accepted Him as our Lord and Savior. Even more exciting, many of my family members followed suit, including my parents. It was truly awesome for me to see my father grow into a wonderful God-fearing man. In fact people who came to learn about our family history before we were saved couldn't believe just how much our lives had changed. Those who knew us before we accepted Christ into our hearts were truly amazed to see what great changes God was making in our lives.

TWO

Witnessing God's Miracles
(1978–1980s)

$\mathcal{I}$ must say, even though Dennis and I had given our hearts to God, we were not immune to life's obstacles, especially when it came to raising a family. However, I know now that it was through the challenges we faced that we had an amazing opportunity to witness God's miracles and share our faith with others. And that we did.

In 1978, when Corey was five years old, we noticed he was making strange doglike sounds while throwing his arms around. So we took him to the doctor to see if something was wrong. The doctor said Corey had Tourette's syndrome—an incurable disease that would affect his nervous system and cause him to lose control. He went on to tell us that there was medication to help control the symptoms, but he strongly urged against our giving it to him if we could bear the noise. He continued to explain to us that a dose of the medicine could be fatal if it was not exactly the amount needed. So, of course, we opted not to give any of the medicine to Corey.

A couple of years later, the disease and its symptoms worsened, which prompted a call from Corey's teacher complaining that he was disturbing the class. We met at the school with his teacher, the school counselor, and a psychologist, and they suggested Corey be placed in the back of the classroom in an enclosure similar to a drum shield used by drummers performing on stage. That was meant to keep

3

other students from being distracted by Corey. But Dennis and I could not allow that.

As his mother I was devastated to see my child laughed at and picked on for something beyond his control. I knew there was absolutely nothing we could do but pray, and so we did—faithfully. Not long after that, God began answering our prayers and the prayers of many others who were praying on our behalf.

One day we received another call from his school asking Dennis and me to meet with them. We both said to each other, "Now what?" Only this time when we met with them, they asked if we had started Corey on some medication. They went on to say they wanted to know how he had improved to the point where his symptoms were barely noticeable.

Dennis explained to the staff that he and I are Christians who believe in the power of prayer, and we knew God can and does heal. And over the course of our time praying for Corey, God answered miraculously. We could tell they did not know how to respond, so they refocused on Corey's improvement over the past months and told us that it was fine if we believed our prayers for Corey's disease had been answered. Regardless, there was absolutely no denying his improvement because they could see it with their own eyes, and we knew it was an opportunity to share the love of Christ.

Another time, when Lance was an infant, he developed asthma. His asthma was so bad Dennis and I often had to rush him to the hospital emergency room so he could be given shots to help him breathe. Sometimes the attacks were so bad the thirty-mile drive to the hospital felt hopeless.

I remember one day in particular, when Lance was three years old, he had a severe asthma attack. I immediately prayed to God asking, *What do I do?* I then proceeded to read and pray over Lance the words of Mark 10:14, "Let the children come to me, and do not hinder them, for the kingdom of God belongs to such as these." And while I read this I realized in that moment I needed to trust God for Lance's healing, medicine or no medicine. I needed to have full trust in the Lord.

That evening I was shown God's gift of healing. Lance's asthma attack stopped completely and, in fact, he never struggled with it again.

Besides the health challenges of our boys, we also faced financial challenges. In our early years of marriage, Dennis was working construction, and I worked as a nursing assistant. One year Dennis' construction work was slow, which left us struggling to make ends meet. As Christmas time approached, we had hardly any money for food and certainly none to buy gifts for our boys. With the little money we did have, we continued to be faithful in our tithing and giving to God.

A few nights before Christmas Eve, there was a knock on our door. We opened the door, and there stood our pastor with boxes of food and gifts for the boys. I was so overcome with emotion that after he left I ran into the bedroom, got down on my knees, and wept, thinking, *Thank You God for Your faithful provisions!* During those times I realized God was working in our lives to help us come to trust and rely on Him for everything. And as it turned out, He was preparing us for what was to come.

THREE

Dennis
(EARLY 1990s)

$\mathcal{D}$uring the early 1990s Dennis started displaying signs of exhaustion. He would tell me, "It's because I'm getting older."

And I would remind him, "You're only in your forties."

Then one day he found a lump on his neck. Having worked in the medical field, I knew enough to be concerned. So I urged Dennis to go see a general physician, who then referred him to an ear, nose, and throat (ENT) doctor. When Dennis got to the ENT doctor's office, the doctor assessed his symptoms and told him he thought it was a severe sinus infection. He then gave Dennis some antibiotics and sent him on his way. That was all Dennis wanted to hear.

As time went on, though, the lump grew to the size of a golf ball, and I became worried. I started nagging him to go back to the doctor, but all I got back was his excuse that the doctor said it was just a sinus infection.

Ten months later Dennis finally went back to see the ENT doctor. While there the doctor assessed him more carefully than before, noticing Dennis' lymph nodes were enlarged under his arms. The doctor went on to tell him that the lump on his neck could possibly be a tumor. When Dennis explained to him that he had no health insurance except his Veteran's Administration (VA) coverage, the doctor abruptly left the room and never returned. Dennis was left waiting so long that he finally just left.

After that appointment we decided to go to the VA hospital and have some tests done to determine the cause of Dennis' symptoms. The results showed that Dennis had service-related, non-Hodgkin's lymphoma and would need surgery. The doctor was surprised, however, that Dennis had cancer only in his neck region. Apparently that was very unusual for that type of cancer.

As Dennis prepared for surgery, he had to shave off his beard. When he finished shaving, and we both looked at his reflection in the mirror, a panic-stricken fear overcame me. There was not just one tumor on his neck, but there were several more under his chin that we had not noticed before. With the surgery already scheduled, we knew we had to trust God for the outcome.

Unfortunately, as the surgeon tried to remove the tumor, it began to break apart, so they had to stop. The doctors decided Dennis needed to undergo radiation treatments instead. Over the course of six weeks, he received five treatments. He became very ill during that time and lost more than twenty pounds. We were told his saliva glands were burned from the radiation treatment and would not return. Dennis' only option then was using artificial saliva drops and prayer for his glands to be restored. And that is what he and I did, and by the grace of God his glands were restored!

After recouping from the radiation treatments, Dennis began feeling normal again. It was not until a couple years later that the cancer recurred, and he had to start chemotherapy. The treatment the second time required him to take a low dose of chemo orally, which he did for several years to follow. Our prayers for healing were answered as the cancer fell into remission.

FOUR

The Calling
(LATE 1990s)

*D*uring the late 1990s Dennis and I had faithfully been serving God in our home church for many years and attending church services four times a week. While I could see the Holy Spirit was moving our church congregation and community, I had a gut feeling that we needed to be doing more beyond our church walls.

By 1999 I had been a believer for nineteen years. Over the course of those years, I was privy to the amazing things God had done in my life from the healings of loved ones, family salvations (the greatest, in my eyes), and supernatural provisions when we desperately needed help. But as grateful as I was for everything the Lord had done in my life, I still felt something was missing.

I began to pray and fast, asking God to please show me the heartbeat of the church through Jesus' eyes. As I did He answered my prayers by placing a heavy burden in my heart for orphans, widows, and the poor throughout the world. With that newfound burden, I started crying out to the Lord on their behalf for hours each day.

During that time a friend asked me to go with her to an Aglow International Convention in Florida. I initially thought it was too expensive and that Dennis may not be all right with the idea, even though he had always supported whatever I wanted to do. After declining my friend's invitation, I could not seem to get the thought of that opportunity out of my mind. I spoke with Dennis about it and asked for his thoughts. He said, "Why don't you go?" His reaction immediately changed my mind and prompted me to call my friend and tell her I was in.

The time came, and off we went. While there were several good speakers at the convention, nothing touched me quite like Caroline Cox's presentation on "The Slaves of Sudan." As Caroline spoke about the atrocities taking place, she showed horrifying images of women and children in the southern region of Sudan who had been captured by the Arab North and sold into slavery. Her ministry's goals were to take money into those dangerous areas and purchase freedom for the women and children held in slavery. The areas Caroline spoke of were in ruins. They had been bombed, and the water wells were poisoned, making living there nearly impossible. As she continued to share about children being put into sacks and thrown alive into the Nile River and women whose breasts were being cut off so they could no longer breastfeed their babies, I began to weep.

After we left that afternoon, I could not stop crying and thinking about the pictures of those children. Later that evening we attended another session on the "Holiness of God." As we listened to the speaker, I found myself on my knees crying and thinking about the Sudanese children and how they were suffering. I did not seem to notice the twelve thousand women around me, because it felt it was just God and me, so I cried out loud to Him, "God, what can I do?"

His answer was loud and clear: *sell everything you have and give it to the poor.*

I could not believe what I had just heard. Not knowing what to do next, I returned to the hotel room with my friends thinking, *How am I going to tell my husband what has happened?*

Once we got back to Wisconsin, I pondered for more than a week about what God had said. Finally I worked up enough courage to tell Dennis about my experience at the conference.

His first comment to me was, "Why were you the only one to hear this from God out of the twelve thousand women that were there?"

I could not answer his question, but I knew what had happened to me was real, very real.

As time went on, the thought of the Sudanese children pressed on my heart heavily. I would pray, "God, many people are criticizing Caroline for what she's doing, freeing those children only to be captured again and resold. But at least she is doing something!" And while I knew she was doing more than most, I knew there had to be another answer to that need. As I continued to pray and seek the Lord's guidance, it became apparent to me that we would one day have an orphanage in Sudan to help raise those children who had been orphaned as a result of the civil war between the North and South.

After sharing with Dennis about what I felt the Lord was saying to me, he was not receptive at first. I'm one of those people who is always looking for adventure, so he thought, of course, this was just another one of my wild whims. So I continued praying and fasting, knowing that if it was God's will for Dennis and me, He would change Dennis' heart.

Eager to learn more on the subject, I would sit for hours in front of my computer, reading everything I could about Sudan. The more I read, the more I felt a strong pull for me to go to Sudan and see for myself if it was indeed as bad as I had seen and heard.

At the time I was serving as both the children's pastor and school administrator for our church in Pound, Wisconsin. One day the mother of one of my students came up to me and said, "I hear you have a burden for Sudan." After we talked for a while, she gave me contact information for a person she knew who was working for a ministry in Yei, Sudan. I gladly took the information she gave me and called the ministry contact, thinking I might possibly go to Sudan and see for myself all that I had been researching.

Just a few months later I got a call from the ministry in Yei, informing me they had an opening for me to visit them in Sudan that July, which was just three months away. Unfortunately, Dennis had prior work commitments and was not going to be able to go, but he was okay with my going. So I found four friends from our church to go with me, and we headed to Yei, Sudan, not knowing anyone there or the language.

FIVE

My First Trip to Sudan
(1999–2000)

$\mathcal{Y}$ei happens to be in the very southern part of Sudan where the war was happening. To get there we had to fly from Entebbe, Uganda, to Arua, which is in northern Uganda, in a small plane that had to land on a dirt airstrip in the middle of the bush. At our first stop I looked out the window of the plane and saw several soldiers with AK-47s.

The few people on the plane started to get out, so we followed. There were no signs or markings anywhere, and we did not know if we were in Arua or not. It was the blind leading the blind. None of us spoke any Arabic, so we simply stood there beside the runway smiling, our hearts beating like crazy in that unfamiliar territory. When everyone got back into the plane, we followed, and it flew us to our next destination. That time it was Arua. When we landed there we did not know anyone and did not know who exactly would be picking us up. I had only been told some African would come for us. We were quite relieved when he arrived. We learned his name was Lovemore, and while he did speak English, it was very hard for us to understand him. After our introductions, Lovemore piled our luggage on top of his Land Cruiser, and we all loaded up and headed for what turned out to be a long journey to Yei.

At the beginning of the car ride, Lovemore told us he had to stop for a few items he needed from Uganda before we continued. When he got to where he needed to stop, he got out of the truck, and left us five women in a strange place with everyone looking at us. Suddenly a young man came up and laid his hands on the hood of Lovemore's Land Cruiser. He then proceeded to the passenger side of the truck where one of my friends was sitting. With a piercing look, the man continued to stare us down. I was scared to death thinking, *How in the world am I going to live among these people when I have so much fear?* So I said a silent prayer, asking God to help me overcome my fear. Meanwhile my friend sat there as cool as a cucumber. Trying not to appear frightened, I could not help but shout, "Shut the window, shut the window!" In a matter of a few minutes the man went on his way.

When Lovemore got back to the truck, we asked him why the young man had put his hands on the truck as he had. Lovemore explained that when the locals see something nice and they want to have it as well, they lay their hands on it, and supposedly they will eventually get it.

As we traveled over the long, bumpy road to Yei, we crossed the Sudanese border where there were soldiers everywhere. My fear intensified. As we finally got through and were heading down the road to Yei, Lovemore told us how the Sudan People's Liberation Army (SPLA) had freed the town from the Arabs just a year and a half before. He went on to share with us that the aftermath of that conflict had left thousands of dead bodies lying on the roads, which were driven over as the road continued to be in use. He said if we looked closely we could still see remnants of clothing on the road. As I thought of all the soldiers who had shed their blood for that freedom, my heart sunk. What a price they'd had to pay!

In that moment I could not help but thank God for my being born in America. I thought of those children who did not ask to be born in Sudan, but there they were living where heartbreak surrounded them and tomorrow was uncertain. I thought, *What can I do for them?*

Once we got to Yei, we had to stop and get official documents that allowed us to be there. When we went into the document office, one of the soldiers asked me, "What are you doing here?"

I told him I had heard about all the orphaned children and wanted to see if we could help. With tears in his eyes he said, "Preach the light to my people." In a room filled with AK-47s, he gave us their blessing.

Shortly after that I was asked to preach at the local Presbyterian Church pastored by Bishop Elias Taban. Bishop Elias is the head of the Evangelical Presbyterian Church (EPC) in that region. When we got to the church, it had the appearance of a true local church with a grass roof and dirt floors. As I entered I noticed the pulpit was made of tree trunks and stood five feet tall, and the seats were made of trees that had been sawn in half. I was a bit nervous preaching because I had never had a translator for my sermon before. It was an experience for which I was going to have to completely rely on God.

I decided to preach about how the Lord delivered me from a life of alcohol and abuse. When I finished we had an altar call, and ten people decided to come forward to either give their hearts to Christ or rededicate their lives to Him. As I looked into their faces, my heart stirred. I sent up a huge thanks to the Lord for blessing my witness that afternoon.

After church we went to lunch with a pastor and some other folks who were also staying in the same compound we were. I remember how nervous my friends and I were about how our stomachs would handle Sudanese food. After all, my friends and I had heard some strange things about the eating habits of the Sudanese people.

As we took our seats, the pastor sat directly across from me. Once we got our food, some bugs had flown onto my plate, so I started to try and scrap them off. Then suddenly the pastor reached out his hand and grabbed one of them, pulled its wings off and ate it! *It was a termite!* I immediately looked at him, holding back a gag that was rising in my throat and thought, *What in the world are you doing?* He then explained to us that those are a delicacy in their region and then proceeded to reach out for several more, watching our facial expressions as he ate them. Surprisingly enough, termites aside, my friends and I ended up liking the food more than we had anticipated. However, one of my friends did get food poisoning, which was not surprising considering there was no electricity at the time. It was commonplace for restaurants to purchase meat that had been hanging in over 100-degree heat in the market. To prevent getting food poisoning, I learned the meat has to have the daylights fried out of it and be blessed before it's eaten!

During the course of our lunch, we were asked to visit some schools and a hospital to share the gospel of Christ. We were happy to do so. When we first got to the local hospital, I asked, "What would you like us to do?" They excitedly replied, "Preach the Word!" So we did.

Next we went to several schools, and again I asked, "What would you like us to do?" And again, we were told, "Preach the Word of God." So we did.

I was amazed that we had so much liberty to share the Word wherever we were. What an opportunity! It was then I realized that the harvest there was truly ripe, but the laborers were few.

Just as we were leaving one of the schools, the children started running down the road after our vehicle. That's when I saw the face of a little girl in a checkered dress—a vision I will never forget. I knew in my heart at that moment that I would do something for those children.

Six

The Answer

(2000–2001)

*O*n returning to the States, I was asked to share with our church what I had experienced in Sudan. As I prepared for that presentation, I did something that surprised everyone, including me! I resigned as children's pastor, knowing that somehow I needed to start raising funds for an orphanage we would one day have in Yei. I continued as school administrator until the year was up and then resigned from that position as well.

During that time Dennis continued to struggle with the idea of going to Sudan. So I asked God, *If You are calling me, are You not calling my husband, too, since we are one?* Then I prayed this simple prayer: *God, if this burden is not from You, but is of my flesh, please remove it. If it is from You, let it burn!*

Shortly after that time, Dennis came to believe that the Lord was calling us to Sudan. As we prepared to go, Dennis had a routine check-up at the doctor's office for his cancer treatment. The doctor discovered that Dennis' blood count was getting too low, so he told Dennis to stop taking the oral chemo medicine he had been taking for several years. I could not help but be concerned about the idea of our moving to Sudan, knowing they did not have the type of medical facilities to care for Dennis' needs. So we prayed, *God, if You are calling us, You're going to take care of us. And if we die, isn't that what we, as Christians, live for?* That's when it dawned on us that the provisions from God are greater than any obstacle, and we were going to Sudan.

In February 2001 Dennis and I started our own 501(c)(3) nonprofit ministry, calling it Harvesters Reaching the Nations. It is a nondenominational organization working with all believing churches. We decided to use Nations in our name because we felt then and still feel God is calling us to serve children in more nations than just Sudan.

However, our journey to Sudan has not been without criticism. Some people think we should have done it the "right way" and partnered with an already established ministry rather than starting our own. But we strongly felt it was about doing it God's way, and that was the way He led us. I believe that instead of copying other ministries and revivals of others, we need to find out what God wants *us* to do and go for it. We should not compare ourselves to others but instead let God be God in our lives.

In April 2001 Dennis left for Yei, and I was to follow him there in June. Our prayer before he left was that he would know which land to take when he stepped foot on it. When Dennis met with local officials, they showed him different pieces of land where we could build an orphanage and school for God. After visiting the different areas, the village elders decided to give us ninety acres of fertile land with teak and mango trees. At that moment Dennis knew his feet were touching the land that was to be taken for God and His precious children.

SEVEN

First Experiences
(2001)

Our adventures in Sudan have provided us with countless opportunities to strengthen our faith, see God at work firsthand, and experience life in a whole new way. When I arrived in Yei in June of 2001, three months after Dennis first arrived, Dennis had already set up our temporary living quarters across the road from where we would be building our campus. My first night there I walked into the room where we were to stay and saw a rat scurry across the floor. So naturally I let out a scream! Dennis said to me, "Then what are you doing here?"

I knew he wasn't being sarcastic with me; he was merely reminding me that God had called us there, and we were going to have to adjust to those new experiences. And adjust we had to do. There were many evenings when I had to get up in that rat-infested room in the middle of the night, in the dark, and walk through a patch of corn with a flashlight to use the latrine. I was scared to death, especially of the critters that looked like crickets exposed to radiation. I mean these were big crickets and unlike the ones we have in the U.S. They had extremely long legs and could jump like you wouldn't believe. I'd often try to hold my bladder at times but could only do it for so long. Eventually, I made myself get up and walk in the dark to the latrine.

Now that Dennis and I were there together, we were ready to get started on the plans for the campus. Our son, Lance, twenty-four years old at that time, along with some friends came over to help us for three months.

Dennis and Lilly a Few Months After Arrival

What a joy it was to have our son working alongside us! He was a tremendous help to Dennis, and while he felt God was calling him to full-time ministry, he was not sure what that entailed. That was going to have to be something he had to figure out in God's time. In the meantime, while Dennis could teach and train our friends and workers how to build, we all ended up learning many things about building from the locals, such as how to make bricks from the soil on our land.

Not long after we began building on our site, a man came to us because he had heard we were building an orphanage. The man brought with him his newborn baby boy, asking us to take him. As difficult as it was for me, I had to tell him we were not yet open and unable to take his son. He then thanked me and began to walk away. My heart sank. A week later the same man came back with the child wrapped in a piece of torn sheet. He explained that his wife had died in child-birth, he had no job, and his baby had been living off sugar water from a spoon for two weeks now. As I looked at the lifeless body of the child in his father's arms, I began to say a silent prayer, *God, are we supposed to take in this child?*

Deeply pained for the father, I knew that if we didn't take the child, the tiny boy had no chance of living. So I took the weak, nameless baby from the father's arms, bringing him close against my body, and watched the father walk away and slowly disappear.

Soon after, we found out that there were no places to buy diapers or clothing for him. So I worked with what we had and cut up several of our shirts and made diapers, and we used full shirts for blankets. As time went by and Dennis and I looked at this tiny baby, we began to bond with him. It was in one of these moments that I glanced at Dennis, a dear man whose heart was so in tune with God, and asked, "Shall we call him Caleb?"

In the Bible, Caleb was one of the spies Moses sent to scope out the Promised Land. He was a brave forty years old at the time. When the spies returned, they put fear into the hearts of the people, telling them that giants populated the land. But Caleb trusted the Lord and declared, "Let us go up at once, and possess it, for we are well able to overcome it" (Numbers 13:30), and he assured Moses they should go into the land. For that Moses promised Caleb, "The land on which your feet have walked will be your inheritance and that of your children forever, because you have followed the LORD my God wholeheartedly" (Joshua 14:9). His story is told in the books of Numbers and Joshua. As told in the book of Joshua chapter fourteen, at the age of eighty-five, Caleb gave his full testimony to God's faithfulness, and his faith was still unwavering. While the land Caleb inherited still had giants, Caleb knew the Lord would help conquer them.

I love the Bible's account of Caleb. At the time I especially felt that Caleb's story represented the faith we needed to recognize that the Lord would help us with that precious infant both now and as he continued to grow into a young boy. So Dennis and I agreed the little boy should be called Caleb.

Weighing in at less than two kilos (about four pounds), we knew Caleb's journey was going to be difficult. We placed Caleb's bed, which was one of our washbasins with a mosquito net over it, on the floor next to our bed. That was going to be his little nest until he outgrew it. While it wasn't exactly like a baby's nursery we would find in the States, little Caleb did not seem to mind. In fact the surroundings were far better than anything the Sudanese homes had at the time.

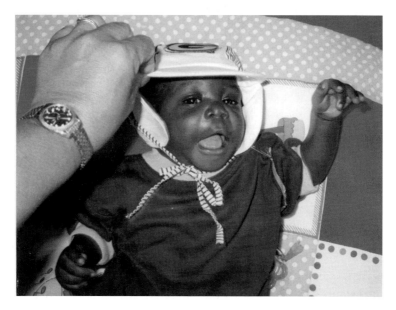

Caleb at Four Months

Over the course of the next several months, Dennis, Lance, our friends, and the locals we hired started to build the dormitories so we would have a place to live. Once they had one of the dorms near completion with a flushing toilet, we moved right in.

During that time I hired a cook to feed the helpers. The cook would build a makeshift grill and cook over firewood burning on the ground. For Dennis and me, we purchased a camp-style propane stove and cooked on that. And for baby Caleb, depending upon the weather and road conditions, we would drive between six to ten hours to Arua, Uganda, to buy him formula and other baby items. A few months later we met some locals in town who were making beds with hand tools, so we decided to draw a picture of a baby bed for Caleb and have one made.

Dennis and Lance Building First Dorm in 2001

By October 2001 we had taken in ten orphans to live with us in the dorm in addition to Caleb. One of the first children was a fourteen-year-old boy named James Ladu. James was originally from the Terekeka region, but when his village was ambushed during the civil war, he was separated from his family. In 2001 he was rescued by a passing aid worker and brought to Yei to an organization across from where our campus is now. Eventually the organization he was staying with closed, and they asked if we could take him. So we did.

James, our oldest orphan at that time, was quite helpful, but it was not enough. The work it took to care for all the children became more than I could manage on my own, so I decided to hire a local Sudanese woman by the name of Itiya (EE-tee-ya). She was our first housemother. Itiya came to us from a small village just behind Harvesters' property in Yei. As we got to know her more, we learned that she used to struggle with alcohol and did not know the Lord. We also learned that her husband and three kids, along with her mother and some of her other relatives, still lived in that small village. Since job opportunities are limited in the Sudanese culture, it is not uncommon for the able body in the household to take a

First Orphans, October 2001

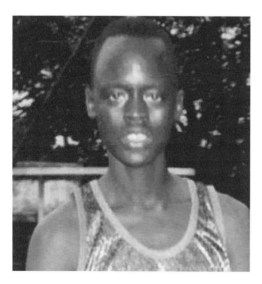

Ladu, Early Years

job away from their home in order to provide for their family.

"Mama Itiya," as she is known, was able to help with the responsibilities I had, such as cleaning Caleb's diapers and clothing. That required a small basin filled with hot water, which had to be heated by firewood in a fifty-five-gallon drum. Until we got the staff living quarters completed, Mama Itiya stayed with us in a spare room so she could help with Caleb and the other children.

I'll never forget one of my first experiences with bats was with Mama Itiya. One night she and I were sitting in a room when bats started flying around us. Itiya immediately hit the floor and crawled under a table, while I screamed and tried

Mama Itiya

to hit the bats as they flew over my head. The guards nearby heard our screams and came running. Despite the fact that the guards were drunk at the time, they attempted to help us by grabbing pieces of bamboo and swatting at the bats. But it was apparent to me that there was no way the guards were going to successfully hit the bats, so I opened the door, and the bats finally flew out. Thank God!

Since mango trees surrounded our campus, and since bats love mango trees, they seemed to be everywhere, crawling on the couch, floor, and walls. This was not one of the adventures I was expecting in Sudan. At times Dennis and I felt surrounded, so we became quite good at *batminton,* if you know what I mean!

EIGHT

Matthew Stephen
(2001)

*B*efore I went to Sudan, I thought our decisions to accept orphans would be easy decisions to make. They would come in, be well fed and taken care of, grow, and prosper. Little did I know that would not always be the case.

One day during our first year in the dorm with Caleb and the other children, our guard came to us and told us that there was a man sitting across the road under the mango tree who wanted to see us. Dennis decided to go over first. When he got there he found a man with no legs sitting in a wheelchair. It turned out another man had pushed him in his wheelchair more than three miles to our campus on very rugged roads. The man in the wheelchair told Dennis that he and his wife had been bombed in the local market in Yei by one of the Antonov planes from the North, which is how he lost his legs.

He went on to say that his wife had died three weeks earlier from starvation and alcoholism, which left him with a three-week-old son he had no means to care for. As the man shared his story, Dennis could tell he was bitter and struggled with alcoholism himself. He then asked Dennis if we would take his son into our orphanage.

Dennis asked, "Where is he?"

The man proceeded to lift his hand and open a piece of rag in which the child was lying. By that point I had come over to see what was going on, and that's when Dennis looked at me uncertainly and asked, "Have you seen the baby yet?"

I replied, "No."

He said, "Don't look unless you're going to take him in."

As I looked and saw this small child's skeleton with little flesh on it, I thought, *How in the world can we take this child in when we do not have enough staff to manage the children we currently have?*

I reluctantly told the man the same as I had told Caleb's father, "We don't have enough help right now."

He looked straight at me and said, "If you don't take this child, I will just throw him down and let him die."

I honestly didn't know what to do, so I gathered the child in my arms and took him to the nearest hospital in Yei. When we first arrived, they weighed the child in at 1 kilo, which is 2.2 pounds. He really was tiny. The doctor said to me, "I think he may live if you keep him warm and feed him with a syringe." Unfortunately, the following morning he died, and I ended up having to do one of the hardest things I've ever had to. I took the baby, which we named Matthew Stephen, wrapped his body in a towel, and went to look for his father in town. When I finally found him, he was drunk and wanted nothing to do with his child's body. It is customary for Africans to want to bury the body of a family member, but he was not interested.

At first I questioned, *Lord, why would You bring this child into our lives so early in the ministry and let him die?* I had truly believed in my heart he would live. As sad as I was, I realized God always has a better, often different, plan than mine. As I pondered that for a while, I could feel the Holy Spirit say to me, *You gave him the human touch and love he didn't have for the three weeks of his short life. You also gave him a name and proper burial.*

We knew tiny precious Matthew Stephen was in a better place with our Lord in heaven, and this put peace in my heart. Several weeks after baby Stephen passed, his father began to visit our Sunday morning church service that we held under a mango tree. After several weeks of attending, he came forward and gave his heart to Christ. A week or two later he disappeared, and we never saw him again. But we do know God knows where baby Stephen's father is and that he was attracted by Jesus' love, demonstrated in the quiet ministrations of what we were able to do for him and his child. Looking back I realize that occurrences like that are what brought us to Sudan. As Jesus says in Matthew 25:40, "Inasmuch as you did it to one of the least of these . . . you did it to Me." (NKJV)

Matthew Stephen's Grave

NINE

God's Healing Touch over Me
(2001)

*O*ver the years we've learned that illnesses are opportunities for building our faith, developing perseverance, and demonstrating the power of prayer and God's healing touch. Before we had water faucets on our campus, I had to carry water in "jerry cans," which hold about five gallons of water, from the borehole where the pump was, to our house twenty yards away. Not only did I have to carry them, but I also had to lift them chest high in order to pour the water into the basin I used for bathing. After doing this for several months, I pulled some ligaments in my right forearm. Since I did not have access to an arm sling, I made my own from a torn sheet. I knew I would have to make do at the time until I could get the injury addressed during an upcoming visit to the States.

Before getting back to the States, one day I went walking down the road and unaware strolled right into fire ants. When I realized what I had done, I panicked and began stomping my feet until I fell forward on the road. While I was able to brace myself with my right hand, I had unfortunately pulled my thumb all the way back, dislocating it from its socket. As painful as it was, I had to push it back into the socket and have Dennis duct tape it down on my palm so it could heal. Between the ligaments and my thumb, the use of my right arm was quite painful.

Another time some of Dennis' laborers were working in the bush putting up a *tukul* (hut) for some of our live-in employees. I walked over to see how things were going. As I was standing in the knee-high elephant grass, talking to the men, I suddenly felt a burning, pinching sensation on my lower legs and feet. I suddenly realized I was standing on an anthill, so I began to scream and jump around. All the men started to laugh at me as I ran toward the house, trying to shake the ants off my legs. After I got to the house, I saw that my legs were bleeding from all the bites, and I knew fire ants in Africa are no joke!

A few months later I was scheduled back in the States to do some fundraising for our ministry. My itinerary for the day consisted of four back-to-back meetings. Once my plane touched down in Texas, a dear friend of mine, Sharon "Shay" Buttolph, founder of Children of War—Children of Hope, and her husband, Dan, picked me up at DFW Airport in Dallas, and we drove for about half an hour to their home in Weatherford, Texas. By the time we reached their house, I had begun to run a fever. The fever was then followed by body aches and vomiting. I had to go to bed. Shay immediately got on the phone, canceled all my speaking engagements for the day, and proceeded to care for me for the next several days until I was feeling better. Once I felt up to it, I headed back to my hometown in Wisconsin, frustrated that I had to cancel all of my meetings and still was not feeling well.

Once I got home, I called my doctor's office and made an appointment for a physical. I had several tests done at the beginning of the week and did not hear back from the doctor by Friday, so I thought all must be well. Sunday night rolled around and the phone rang. It was my doctor. I knew it must be serious if she was calling me on a Sunday. She informed me that my blood liver count came back 420 times higher than normal and that the CT scan taken of my liver showed a lump the size of a lime next to my heart. She went on to say I needed to have more testing done.

That was torturous for me, because all I could think about was the dreaded C word—*cancer*. At that time I also found out the symptoms I'd had in Texas were signs of chronic malaria. I reached out to some friends who are real prayer warriors and asked them to pray a prayer of healing over me before my next doctor's appointment.

When I got to my next appointment, the doctor performed an ultrasound over and around my heart to detect the lump that was seen in the previous scan. Only that time she did not find anything! So I gladly packed my bags and went home to Sudan confirmed in knowing that God was once again faithful in His care of me.

TEN

Growing Pains
(2002)

$\mathcal{I}$n preparation for starting the orphanage, school, and church, we began outfitting the campus by collecting items and storing them in a warehouse back in the States. Once we had a container full of items, we had to ship it to Sudan.

Since that was our first experience with a container, we did not realize how involved the process would be. To help get us started, many folks back home, including some local elementary schools, joined together to coordinate the collection of items. In order to get these items to Sudan we had to ship them via ocean freight, which required us to either rent or purchase a container to transport our goods. We decided it would be best to purchase a forty-foot container that was eight feet tall by eight feet wide so we could then use it for storage on the campus.

Throughout the process, an inventory log and the proper paperwork for customs had to be created and shipped with the container. Once the container was packed to its brim, it was picked up and shipped to its first destination—Mombasa, Kenya. From there it would be trucked to our campus in Sudan. Given that Yei was a warzone at the time, it made finding a trucking company willing to bring it to our campus rather difficult. Not only that, the roads were so terrible we were not quite sure when we could expect the container to arrive. After finding a willing trucking company, we waited patiently for the container's arrival.

Three months after the container's initial departure, it arrived on our campus atop the truck that had brought it from Mombasa, Kenya, to Yei, Sudan. After the truck pulled onto our campus, the doors opened, and we systematically unloaded everything. Our next step was to get the container unloaded off the truck bed. That was a process in itself. To start, the Ugandan driver had to tie the container to a big teak tree with a chain. He then got back into his truck and proceeded to hit the gas pedal. After several failed attempts, the truck driver realized he had forgotten to unlock the container locks from the truck bed. So he unlocked them, got back in his truck and pressed the gas pedal, which allowed the container to easily drop off. By that time nightfall was fast approaching, so we had to hurry to get the items we wanted to store back into the container and locked away to avoid theft.

Offloading Container

At that time our orphanage was housing fifty children. With that type of growth, our primary objective with construction was to focus on the completion of the second dormitory for the children and living quarters for our staff and ourselves. Since we did not have any classrooms to teach school in yet, we chose to hold the classes under the mango trees, because they provided ample shade and some temperature relief long enough to hold gatherings for a few hours at a time. We also did not have a church built at that time, so we held church under the mango trees as well.

Teacher and Class Under the Mango Tree

Despite all our progress, I began to struggle with being discouraged by the difficult circumstances we were encountering regularly. I knew God had called us, but life in Sudan was, quite frankly, hard to adjust to. One week in particular nearly broke me. We had just lost two orphan babies to malaria and received bad news from back home that Dennis' niece had died from cystic fibrosis. By then all I could do was sit on our front stoop and cry, feeling sorry for myself. I must confess that I was having a pity party. Not only did we not have enough money to go back home for his niece's funeral, but we both could not leave the campus together. At the time we were dealing with some disloyalty from some of our local staff, and our funds were running low. So in theme with my pity party, I began to complain to the Lord. In the midst of my complaints, I felt the Lord nudge my heart to look at Jeremiah 12:5, which says, "If you have raced with men on foot and they have worn you out, how can you compete with horses? If you stumble in safe country, how will you manage in the thicket by the Jordan?" When Jeremiah called to God for relief, His reply was essentially, "If you think this is bad, what are you going to do when things really get hard?" I was reminded then that not all answers to our prayers are comforting. But I knew I needed to be committed to Him even when things don't go the way I had planned or when He answers my prayers in His timing and not mine. Honestly though, I thought I had a pretty good reason to complain since we were living in a war-torn land, in the bush with bomber planes flying over us daily, and essentially cut off from the outside world. Yet God rebuked me and my pity party, quickly reminding me of how I had sat and cried, asking Him to use me, and now that He was, I had the nerve to complain. I repented to the Lord and began praising Him instead for His faithfulness.

ELEVEN

Life on the Road in Sudan
(2002)

$\mathcal{R}$oad trips throughout Uganda and Sudan ended up providing us with many adventures to come. It took us our first year of living in Yei to realize just how important having a vehicle would be for our growing orphanage and school. We had wanted to use what little money we brought with us for building dorms for the children. To save cost on building materials, we sought local woodsmen to take the indigenous lumber and cut it down to size. It took two men to do that process, one in a hole and one above the hole, using a large double-bladed saw in a teamwork fashion to slide the saw back and forth. We'd then hire large lorries (trucks) to deliver the wood, building supplies, and other items we needed.

The locals, however, thought it strange that we did not have a vehicle. When Dennis had to walk more than three miles into town, the locals would ask him on his walk, "Where is your vehicle?" and he would reply, "I don't have one." What we learned is, it was uncommon for locals to see any white person without a vehicle, which explained why Dennis kept getting strange looks.

Once the orphanage and school were up and running, it made sense to have a vehicle. Being familiar with the conditions of Sudan's roads, we knew we would need a truck that could handle the rough terrain. So we decided to order a Land Cruiser from a dealership in Kampala, Uganda. In order to get the vehicle, Dennis had to travel 435 miles to Kampala. As he made his way there, he ended up having to sleep outside near the Sudan/Ugandan border for several nights with no mosquito net. Over the course of his trip, Dennis began to feel sick with aching joints, fever, headache, backache, blood in his urine, and he began to lose his vision in his left eye. He knew something was wrong, but he did not get any medicine in Uganda because he thought he could ride it out. Due to the difficulty of customs in Africa, it took Dennis nearly three weeks to return to Yei with the new vehicle. When Dennis finally got to our campus, it was 11:30 p.m. He got out of the vehicle, and I could tell he was sick. As he started to walk into the house, he said, "I have never been this sick in all my life, not even when I had cancer." I knew it had to be serious because Dennis is not one to complain. By the next morning, Dennis was worse, so I took him to a German doctor in the area who was working for six months at the leprosy and TB hospital.

When we got there the doctor assessed Dennis and ran some tests. The results showed that Dennis had malaria. We told the doctor we had been taking malaria medicine since we first got to Sudan as a preventative measure, but he informed us that, unfortunately, there are several kinds of medicine that no longer work for the region where we were living. Fortunately for us the doctor said he had the means to treat Dennis' malaria. However, he shared his concern regarding Dennis' past history of lymphoma and recommended that Dennis fly back to the States for some further testing. So we headed to Arua, Uganda, the nearest place to catch a plane at the time.

Once we arrived in Arua, we got a room at one of the local motels. We then went to get some supper before we called it a night. I was feeling fine at the time, so I ordered some fish. It turned out, once I placed my order, one of the restaurant employees had to go to the local market, buy the fish, bring it back, and cook it. Three hours later I had my food. After finishing dinner, we went back to our room. Not long after we got back, I began to feel nauseated with cramps in the pit of my stomach as I'd never felt them before. I ran for the toilet and had severe diarrhea. I started to feel light-headed, so I got up and tried to go back to the bed where Dennis was lying. The next thing I knew, I was waking up on the cement floor next to the bed with Dennis standing over me saying, "Lil, are you okay?"

I answered, "What do you mean? I've been here all night." I seriously thought I was in bed that night.

As Dennis tried to help me up, I yelled, "I have to puke!"

He quickly ran into the bathroom and grabbed the small washbasin for me, and I vomited until there was literally nothing left. We had no ice or washcloths, so Dennis wet a towel and placed it on my head. I wondered if perhaps I had gotten a brain concussion from hitting my head on the cement floor when I fell that night. It turned out I had a bad case of food poisoning. After resting a few more hours, I began to feel better, and I was able to get Dennis on a plane heading home to the States. Thus began my journey back on the long road to Sudan.

One advantage of having a vehicle meant that I didn't have to rely on Dennis to walk to the market and do our shopping for us. After all, now that he was back in the States, I had to do the shopping. My first time at the market, I went to purchase some corn maize. While the corn maize was being ground, I sat and waited in the truck, which I had parked outside the market next to a bamboo fence that was around the grinding mill. As I sat there waiting, several people started to come around the truck. Some were able to speak English, but most did not. It was apparent to me that I stood out like a sore thumb. Being white I drew a lot of attention.

Just then a young boy (about fourteen) came up to me and said, "Mama, I am your son." He was stumbling and not talking very clearly, and I knew he was high on opium. He kept talking and smiling, staggering around the truck. I became increasingly uncomfortable, as I was not quite sure what he was up to. Suddenly he grabbed part of the bamboo fence, pulled it off, and headed for my truck. I thought, *Oh, no! He's going to smash my windows!* Instead he started to swing a large piece of bamboo at anyone who came close to the truck. I then realized he was protecting me, because he thought I was his mother.

My heart stirred for the handsome young boy, who seemed to have no hope in truth. Rather his hope was in alcohol and drugs that offered him only temporary relief from the heartache in his life. So I told him, "Jesus loves you, and so do I."

A few weeks later I went to the market again, this time with Rose, a supervisor in our orphanage, and a couple of our guards. I noticed a crippled man following us, so we began to walk quickly toward my truck. But we were not fast enough. As I tried to open the door, he grabbed my arm. I then swung around and told him to let me go. Even though our guards were close by, they just stood there while this guy was getting rough with me.

Thankfully a Muslim storeowner I knew grabbed me and positioned me behind him. He started to talk to the unruly guy very strongly, but the guy kept yelling and demanding we give him money. As that continued, Rose and I jumped into the truck. For some reason Rose wanted to give him coins, but I knew giving him money only meant he would purchase more alcohol and threaten us more the next time. So I told her no for those very reasons. That particular man had a history in the market of going around and threatening people until he got what he wanted. But that time he was not going to get anything, so he raised his crutch at my truck in an attempt to smash my mirrors. I quickly started the vehicle, and Rose, out of fear, reached into her purse and threw him a coin as we drove off.

However, not all of the excitement happened in the market. One day a local friend and I decided to drive into town with our guard. It had been raining all day, which made it feel as if I was back in Wisconsin driving on ice, *or so I thought!*

At that time military checkpoints were all around Yei. As we approached one of the checkpoints, two big lorry trucks were sitting on top of the hill blocking our way. Because Sudan has the British driving system, I had to pass the vehicles on the right. But in that case, there was no room to do so, and I opted to pass on the left. Just as I started to pass the truck, our guard spoke up saying, "Mama, don't do that."

I replied reassuringly, "Don't worry, I can do it."

Just as I said that, my vehicle started leaning with the slant of the road, and we ended up sliding right into the side of the big lorry. Somehow during the fiasco, the top of our Land Cruiser got caught on the lorry, and neither of us could move. At first I froze thinking, *How am I going to get unhooked from the lorry without damaging our new truck?* To make matters worse I realized I was pinned in the driver's side and could not get out. I decided to roll down my window and holler at the locals who had gathered around my vehicle to tell them to take my hydraulic winch and hook it to a tree. I knew I could maneuver the winch from inside my truck. Knowing our truck was only a few weeks old, I started thinking and saying aloud, "My husband is going to kill me!"

Some of the local men laughed at me and replied, "No, Mama. No. He won't kill you."

As I started to push the button to operate the winch, I could hear cracking and twisting sounds as if my windows were going to pop out. I became so overwhelmed I thought I was going to lose it. In that moment I took a deep breath and prayed. I told myself, *Let's get this truck unhooked and deal with the damages later.* Just as I started to press the button again, several men pushed the side of the truck loose, breaking it free from the lorry.

While that was a huge relief, I couldn't help but think, *What a dumb broad these guys must think I am.* Surprisingly they said to me, "What a brave woman you are!"

I thought to myself, *Not brave, honey, just crazy!*

After we drove away, I stopped to see the damage. I saw there were only a few scratches, and the top of the roof was ever so slightly dented and loose. Other than that all was okay. God is so good!

While continuing to adjust to the rigors of driving in Sudan, I learned some important lessons along the way about life in a war-torn country. At times I would drive several people to town in our truck when suddenly everyone would open their doors, jump out, and run under the trees. The first time that happened, I shouted, "What's going on?"

They shouted back, "The Antonov is coming!"

Realizing I didn't want to be out in the open either, I did my best to hide our truck under the tree and wait with everyone else for the Antonov plane to pass over. Once the plane had passed over us, we all regrouped, loaded back into the truck and were on our way. Those air attacks were apparently part of a relentless campaign by the Sudanese government at that time and had left tens of thousands of innocent civilians dead, injured, or displaced from their communities. It was crazy to think I was now living in the very war zone that at one time I had only heard and read about.

Another time I had to drive some visitors to Arua, Uganda. The trip is only about sixty miles, but I knew it would take us six to ten hours, depending on the weather and the notorious condition of the roads. Because of previous experiences, we always kept a shovel, axe, and hoe in the back of the truck in case we encountered any obstacles on our drive.

During that particular trip we had to make diversions into the bush because of the land mines known to be in the area. Every so often I'd get out and walk the road to check for mines to avoid. After I had checked out the path as best I could, I would get back into the vehicle and drive forward. As we proceeded I held my breath, heart pounding, while pleading the blood of Jesus over the truck in hopes we would not encounter a land mine, and we didn't. We were so thankful our merciful God got us to our destination safely! Occurrences like these were constant reminders that life in Yei, Sudan, was much different than what I was used to at home!

Twelve

A Wartime Experience
(2002)

While Dennis was back in the States, he shared with me that the doctors ran some tests and were going to treat him for his cancer over the next couple of months. One day while he was gone, I drove into town with Rose, Florence (our cook at the time), and one of our armed guards to get some supplies for the orphanage. As we approached a checkpoint, I noticed there was a lorry filled with soldiers in full gear. While it was common to see soldiers, they were typically not decked out in their military gear. So when we saw these soldiers they stood out. As I began to approach the gate our guard yelled, "Mama, don't stop!" But the gate was down, so I had no choice.

Suddenly two men ran up to our car trying to hijack it. As their eyes locked on mine, they took a step back. Just as that was happening, a girl standing near the gate decided to open it, which then prompted me to floor the gas pedal and speed right through the checkpoint. I am not sure what those men saw when they looked at me. It could have been an angel in our midst, or perhaps it was simply my blonde hair, but they backed off, and we were thankful they did!

Not too long after that ordeal, I found out that the group of soldiers in the lorry had shot two men and hijacked their vehicle just before we came through that checkpoint. The Lord's mercy was indeed covering us.

As we headed on into town, we noticed most of the stores were closed, and there were even more soldiers there than usual. I asked a local man what was going on, and he said the soldiers from the South were leaving the frontline and moving through our area. He went on to tell me that the soldiers were hungry and searching for food, and when someone refused to give them what they wanted, they would shoot off that person's feet. He also said they were raping women as they came through.

Rather than continuing on to shop, I headed for the commander's house to ask for extra guards to be stationed at our campus to help protect our orphanage and school. When I arrived he asked if I would take one of his soldiers to the governor's house. I agreed, and leaving Rose and Florence with the commander, the two guards and I went to the governor's house.

Upon trying to return to the commander's house, we entered mass chaos. There was lots of shooting and people running around trying to flee the area. I immediately started driving the truck backward as fast as possible to "get out of Dodge," but I realized I needed to get Rose and Florence from the commander's house before leaving the area completely. I frantically drove down several different roads trying to get out of the range of gunfire and was able to make it back to the commander's place only to find out that Rose and Florence were not there. When I asked where they were, I was told they had been caught directly in the crossfire, and when the shooting stopped for a moment, they got up and ran.

By that time it was dark, and I knew I needed to get back to the orphans at our campus, but they told me it was too dangerous to travel at night. In fact, roadblocks had been put up, and they had arranged for me to stay the evening in town in the guesthouse of the Norwegian People's Aid. As I lay there hearing shooting throughout the night, I kept wondering, *Are our children safe?*

About midnight I heard a knock at the door. It was Bishop Elias. Our guards at the campus had sought him out to see if he knew where I was, since I had not returned. He came to check on me to see if I was safe so he could notify our campus guards of my whereabouts and that I was indeed all right. He went on to reiterate to me that it was still too dangerous for me to leave in the middle of the night; I needed to stay.

When morning came I was able to return to our campus because it was safer to travel in daylight. Arriving at the campus, I was relieved to see that Rose and Florence had been able to make their way back to the campus unharmed as well.

During the next two weeks, the government assigned several extra guards to protect us as the civil unrest continued. At night we would often have to sit silently with the generator off so the soldiers moving down the road would pass us by. Considering we were caring for children on our campus, sitting in silence was certainly no easy task. As all the commotion and strife was going on around me, I couldn't help but feel alone. With Dennis in the States, I was literally the only foreigner for miles around, as far as I knew.

I understood, however, that it was a trying time for the soldiers too. They had been fighting for so long for freedom they were physically and emotionally exhausted and by then just ready to go home. But their journey home was indeed causing a palpable fear among us, and we knew, as hard as it would be, the war was something we were going to have to work through. I could sense my faith and trust in the Lord were being tested as I began experiencing the pain, violence, and death Sudan had been dealing with for decades. In those moments I clung to Isaiah 43 and reminded myself of the Lord's words: "Fear not . . . you are mine . . . I will be with you . . . 'You are my witnesses,' declares the LORD, 'whom I have chosen'" (verses 1, 2, 10).

THIRTEEN

Culture Shock

(2003)

$\mathcal{T}$he first couple of years of living in Sudan exposed me to more than just the typical shock of experiencing a different culture from my own. However, I've been blessed with other missionaries who have traveled alongside Dennis and me. The first to join our team on the ground was a long-term missionary from Malaysia named Guna Pooshani. Pooshani, as we know her, came to us in 2003 to help in the school and later lead the church. She had been working in business in Malaysia when she came to know Jesus Christ as her Savior. She soon felt God directing her into full-time ministry. After finishing Bible college, she specifically felt called to serve in Sudan. That's when her church in Malaysia sent her to Harvesters to help pastor the children, staff, and local community. I was especially grateful to have Pooshani join our ministry, because I felt akin to her since we were both expatriates wanting to serve the Lord in this capacity.

Once Pastor Pooshani was with us, I did not feel so lonely when Dennis had to head back to the States for his doctors' appointments. I remember one time in particular, Dennis was in Wisconsin, and Pooshani and I decided to do some serious fasting because there were many needs for the work at Harvesters. So we gathered one evening in our house with two of our local female employees and spent several hours in worship and prayer. As we were praying and singing, the generator went off, leaving us with just a dimly burning lantern. Then all of a sudden

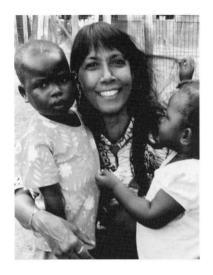

Pooshani

one of our employees I'll call Sally began to yell, "I feel the power, I feel the power!" I first thought she was under the anointing of the Holy Spirit, but then she let out a scream and threw herself back in the chair and was unconscious for about ten minutes. When she came to, she sat staring at the palms of her hands and looking around the room as if she did not know where she was. Then she got up and ran out of the house. Pooshani said, "Mama, we need to go get her."

We ran after her and brought her back into the house. We were astonished at what we saw. Never in all the years of my Christian walk have I seen what I saw that night. Sally's eyes looked lifeless and were filled with darkness. They were glazed over, and she looked like a zombie. She started speaking in different voices. Some were men's voices and some were women's voices. As she stood in the middle of the room, she started quoting John 10, where Jesus talks about our being "His sheep" and that "we know His voice." Then she mocked and bleated like a sheep, shouting other Bible verses while turning in circles. Not only did it appear to be demonic behavior, but the demons knew the Word of God, and that was exactly what the Bible tells us can happen.

So Pooshani and I began to pray over her for more than five hours, asking God to give us the wisdom and faith to cast the demons out of her. Finally, when Sally calmed down, we took her to the house next to mine so she could rest. After we prayed for some time, I walked Pooshani to her house and then returned to mine. I must admit I was a bit fearful and could not sleep at all. Sally had been living with Dennis and me for more than two years and professed to be a Christian. Yet before my eyes those spirits were manifesting. I became so troubled by the situation that night that I locked myself in my bedroom and prayed, asking God for His help. *I cannot do this without You, Lord! I need Your help!*

Another one of our female employees stayed with Sally that night. The next day that employee informed us that Sally had been vomiting throughout the night. When Sally returned to our house, it was obvious she was not herself. The demons had taken possession of her once again. Her head kept twitching, which was a sight I never imagined I would find on our campus, much less in our house. For the remainder of the day, Sally kept to herself. I knew she needed to be in the Word, so I encouraged her to read the Bible while she sat alone.

Nighttime rolled around again, and Pooshani and I started to worship and pray once more with Sally. As soon as we started praying, Sally was thrown to the floor. At times she got up from the floor, raised her arms, and spoke in a man's voice. During that time I sensed a faith well up inside me, and I knew God was answering my prayers, and I had nothing to fear. For several hours we quoted Scripture and spoke out in faith over Sally. I then proceeded to repeatedly command the demons to come out, and when I did, Sally would sigh aloud and fall to the floor and be freed from one demon to the next. Several demons came out of her that evening, but it took our working four long nights of calling upon the Lord for Him to free her completely.

I was aware some people look for demons under every rock, but we happened to be in the Holy of Holies, and those demons had to go somewhere. I cannot explain those events because Sally claimed to be a Christian. I personally do not believe God and Satan can dwell in the same house, but I saw what I saw. I've learned since that in the Sudanese culture there are many tribal things related to witchcraft they still deal with even as Christians. There are some things we simply cannot explain, and I am not going to try on this one. I just know the people need to be taught and grounded in the Word of God. A few days after that, Pooshani and I were teaching in the school chapel about the Holy Spirit. Again as we were singing and worshipping the Lord, a number of the students began to scream and fall on the floor, rolling around in anguish. People from around the area heard the screams and came running to the campus to see what was happening. That went on for about two weeks. Every time we sang and worshipped the Lord, the kids would fall to the floor.

When we asked the kids what was going on, they each replied differently. Some said they saw Jesus, some saw fire or hell, and others said Jesus spoke to them. It was amazing to see, and I knew it was real because our kids at Harvesters had never seen anything like it. We knew we had to teach them the Word of God. After all, Scripture says when the demons are cast out, if we do not fill that house with His Word, seven more demons will return, and the people will be in worse condition than they were before (see Luke 11:24–26).

Even in our women's ministry demon activity began to happen at that particular time, and many women were delivered from the demons as well. It was and still is important for us not to rejoice about how we can cast out demons, but to rejoice that our names are written in the Lamb's book of life (Luke 10:20, Revelation 21:27).

In addition to these issues, we also experienced superstition in a manner that affected the entire culture. One day one of our workers went to the local market to buy beef for the orphans, but when he returned to the campus he did not have any meat. I asked him why, and he said, "It is being said the meat is coming from Arabs and that if you eat the meat you will turn into a cow." He went on to explain that because of that superstition the local government stopped the selling of meat in the markets. There were even rumors that a woman at the police station was half woman and half cow. When word about her got around, people flocked to the police station to see her.

We faced superstitions not only in the marketplace but also on our own campus. Many times after we worked so hard to educate and teach the children the truth, our housemothers, who were uneducated and often superstitious, told them something different. We even had one of our educated teachers tell some of the students they should not take any medicine from town because it came from the North, and if they took it they would turn into a cow. It seemed like every step forward we made with the kids, we took two steps backward because of how deep superstition runs in the Sudanese culture.

One night in particular the generator ran out of diesel, and the lights started to flicker. The housemothers and orphans all ran for the back door of the dorm screaming and crying. With all the commotion I literally thought someone must have died, but instead I learned they thought there were wizards in the dorm, causing the lights to flicker. With the help of some of the local teachers living on campus, I was able to explain to them why the lights were flickering. However, we were not too successful in convincing them of the truth that night, so we ended up turning off all the lights and giving them a lantern to use instead.

Of the many things God has taught me through these intense events, the most important one I found comfort in is that He is Sovereign. He is Almighty. He is the King of kings and the Lord of lords. "Greater is he that is in you, than he that is in the world" (1 John 4:4 KJV).

FOURTEEN

Almighty Answers
(2003–2004)

*O*ne of the greatest blessings from our time in Sudan thus far had been to see those prayers answered in so many different and unexpected ways among our children at Harvesters, and even in our own family.

In early 2003 a father came to us with his infant son who was sick and weak. He had traveled a great distance from his Dinka tribe village to Harvesters, hoping we could take his son because he could not care for him properly. He explained that his wife had died and that his son would not live if he did not receive help soon. So we took the boy into our care. Over the next few days Obediah, as he was known, became more and more frail. We knew something had to be done, so we took him to the local hospital. However, they did not feel there was anything that could be done to help him, so they did not admit him. We honestly believed Obediah wasn't going to live much longer, so we sent for his father. When he arrived he told us there was nothing he could do and left.

We knew without God's intervention that Obediah would die, so we took him to one of our daily chapel services where we worshipped and prayed to God with the children. Once we brought him into the service, the children proceeded to gather around and began to pray for him. Jehovah Rapha (the LORD who heals) answered the prayers of those children. After that day Obediah was able to receive the nutrition he needed to grow stronger. Obediah is truly a living example of the healing power of God!

During that same time period, Caleb, who had just turned eighteen months old, started getting sick. Our only healthcare option at that time was to take him to the nearest hospital in Yei, which had no running water or electricity. Often, when we admitted Caleb, the hospital had no medicine to give him or needles for IVs, so we had to drive around to little clinics, hoping to find those items. Despite this hospital's lack of resources, they were able to save baby Caleb time and time again.

When Caleb turned two and a half years old, the hospital informed us that something was wrong with his chest and that we needed to take him to Uganda and have his chest x-rayed. When we got to the Ugandan hospital, the doctors examined little Caleb's body and discovered that he had an enlarged heart. They told us we needed to get him to the States as soon as possible or he would not live much longer. Thus we began the long process of obtaining a visa and passport for Caleb to travel back to the States. I must say, as scary as those times were, I recalled Jeremiah 29:11 and repeated it aloud, "'For I know the plans I have for you,'" declares the LORD . . . plans to give you hope and a future.'" And while we knew the little guy was ours to care for and cherish, more importantly we understood he belonged to the Lord, and that his future was indeed safe in God's hands.

By 2004 we were finally able to get a visa from the U.S. Embassy for Caleb. With his visa in hand, I packed our things, and we got on the first flight we could back to the States. Dennis stayed in Sudan to run the campus. Upon arriving I immediately took Caleb to see a pediatric cardiologist at St. Vincent Hospital in Green Bay, Wisconsin, where we ended up spending four long months. During our time at the hospital, the doctor did an echocardiogram test on Caleb, which is a test that uses sound waves to create a moving picture of the heart. That picture is much more detailed than an ordinary x-ray image and involves no radiation exposure. After the test results came back, the doctor informed me that Caleb's heart was not too bad, but he did have some fluid around it. He then advised me to bring Caleb back a year later for a follow-up visit.

During my time back home in Wisconsin, I spent time with my family. I was able to follow up with Lance on what he had shared in 2001 with Dennis and me when he had come to help us in Sudan for three months. At that time he had told us he felt God was calling him into full-time ministry, but he wasn't quite sure what that looked like, so he returned to the States to pray and think about what God was calling him to do.

While Lance and I chatted, he explained that over the past four years he had fallen into the groove of busying himself with the things of the world. Those things were not bad in and of themselves, but it was evident he was not seeking God's direction during that time. He proceeded to tell me that he had bought himself many "toys" but soon grew restless and discontent with the life he was leading. It was at that point he realized God was dealing with his heart.

As Lance and I continued to talk, it became apparent that one thing in particular was causing him to hesitate about going to the mission field. He had a notion that if he was called to the field he had to preach, which was something he did not feel was his gift. What added to this notion was an evangelist who had told him when he was younger, "All are called but few are chosen" and that he was one of the chosen ones. For many years that idea perplexed him because he felt pressured to preach if he served God in the field. After he and I talked, God gave him the clarity he needed to realize that not everyone is called to pastor and preach in the mission field. With that new insight, Lance decided to embrace God's calling to the mission field and come serve with us at Harvesters in Sudan for a while. So he started to get things in order at home and planned a six-week trip to serve with us.

After Caleb and I returned to Sudan, Dennis and I continued a conversation we began when we first got Caleb. From that very first day, we knew we wanted to make him officially part of our family. We quickly learned that adoption is frowned upon in Sudan. But one day we had an opportunity to meet with the staff of Dr. John Garang, who at that time was top leader of the Sudan People's Liberation Army. During our meeting they explained to us that in their culture it is important to keep their children in their respective families and tribal communities. However, they recognized there were literally millions of orphans who were left as a result of the war. So they gave us their blessings and approval for adoption in the South (with some criteria of course). We were thrilled! To get their blessing was a miracle in and of itself.

So God was doing a mighty work in and on behalf of our family. We were in the beginning stages of making Caleb an official member of the Klepp family, and Lance was stepping out in faith to determine God's plan for him. Dennis and I were grateful to have Lance come that fall. It elated us even more to see he was ready to use the gifts God had entrusted to him, one of those marvelous gifts being the ability to build. During his six-week trip with us he ended up committing to God with a heart to serve Harvesters long-term. What a blessing that was!

FIFTEEN

His Merciful Hands
(2005-2006)

*O*ne of the amazing things the Lord continued showing me was His impact in the lives of others. Witnessing His glory and magnificence through the people of Sudan soon became a gift I truly treasured.

In early 2005 a thirteen-year-old boy by the name of Christopher Mungu came to us. He and his parents were refugees who had fled to a refugee camp in the Congo during the war in Sudan. While at the camp, Christopher's parents died from disease, leaving him to move between relatives as they were able to provide. One of those relatives was his brother, who was a soldier. When his brother left to go fight again, it left Christopher with no other options for provision. Somehow Christopher managed to find his way to Harvesters.

Not long after Christopher joined us, we became impressed by his intellect. Not only could he read and write, but he could also speak three different languages. His ability to learn quickly soon landed him as the top student at our school. But one summer night in 2006, Christopher fell into a coma. We knew immediately it was the dreaded meningitis, which is nearly always fatal once the coma phase sets in. We knew the best thing to do was pray, so we called on the children and our prayer partners back in the States to join us in praying fervently for his recovery.

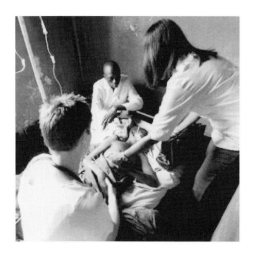

Christopher with Meningitis

Christopher with Visiting Missionary,
Dr. Craig DeLisi

About a week later Christopher came out of his coma, but it was clear that things were not the same. He couldn't recognize familiar faces, his speech was slurred, he had forgotten two of the three languages in which he had been fluent, and his right side was severely weak. It was difficult to accept that our top student was no longer able to read or write. When we touched base with the local hospital, they told us that there was likely permanent brain damage, and many of the side effects we were seeing would remain. So we prayed, and with the merciful hands of the Lord, Christopher started to slowly recover.

Instances such as Christopher's reinforced the importance for us to medically provide for the children. We determined then we needed a building on campus to help provide a place for missionary nurses and visiting medical teams to treat the children. We called this building His Merciful Hands Clinic. One day one of the short-term medical teams that served His Merciful Hands Clinic insisted on seeing what kind of day "Mama Lilly" had when she went to town, so I took two of them with me. However, I was not even expecting the experience we were about to have.

It was a rainy day, and by the time we got to the market area, I could see that there were not many people there. So I parked the Land Cruiser outside the market and entered as I had always done before. I then headed with my visiting friends over to the fruit and vegetable stand to purchase some tomatoes and okra. As I pulled out my wallet to pay, a man came and stood close to me. He didn't say a single word; he just awkwardly stared at me. I became bothered and told him in Juba Arabic to leave, but he ignored my request and continued staring at me. Then, when I least expected it, he reached for and grabbed my $350 bifocals that were hanging on the front of my shirt, smashed them in his hands, and threw them down on the dirt. My two friends froze, and as taken aback as I was, I started yelling at him, wanting in the flesh to haul off and hit him.

I tried to control myself so I could chase him as he began running away. Don't ask me what I would have done had I actually caught him. I could tell the man was drunk, and realizing I wasn't going to catch him, I stopped chasing after him. While that was not my first time being attacked in the market, it was the first time I was left with no glasses with which to see and read well. And of course there was no Walmart nearby to run to for replacements. As furious as I was, I told my friends, "I'm going to the commander's house and have something done."

As we drove off I tried to act like a brave woman, holding back the tears of shock, trying my best to not let them see how really shaken up I was. When we got to the military commander's house, we were met by some of his soldiers and welcomed to enter the house. As I told the commander what had happened to me at the market, he became upset and told his armed guards to go back to the market with me. I thought, *They'll go and talk some sense into the drunken man who destroyed my glasses.*

When we returned to the market, the soldiers jumped out of the truck with their AK-47s and told us to wait by the vehicle. The next thing I saw was strange looks on my friends' faces as we turned around and realized the soldiers were carrying the guy who had attacked me. It appeared as though they had beaten him, or else he was so full of alcohol and drugs he could not walk. As they approached the truck, one of the soldiers told me to open the back door. As that was happening, the rest of the medical missionary team who were visiting pulled up alongside us and asked, "Mama, are you okay?"

Trying to appear brave I answered, "I have just been attacked in the market, but I'm fine." In reality I wanted to run and find a place to sit down and have a good cry, but I had to continue on.

The soldiers threw the man in the back of my truck and told me we needed to take him to the SPLA prison. While the soldiers sat behind my two friends and me as I drove to the prison, I was still a bit nervous that the drunken man in the back was going to jump me while I was driving. But we finally got there and dropped the man off. I was later told they kept the man for a week, roughed him up, and then let him out. When I heard that, I became apprehensive about their decision.

I returned to the market two weeks later and saw the same man in the market. I thought, *Oh no! Here we go again.* But that time was different. He looked at me and yelled, "This is the woman that put me in prison." But he never touched me again. Since then, he has said good morning to me when I visit the market.

Once our medical clinic was built and running successfully, I headed to the States to do some more fundraising for the building of a church and school on our campus. Until then we had been using our dining hall as the chapel and still conducting school under the mango trees. While in the States, our board members and I created the Solomon Project to raise funds for the school buildings. We were also blessed to have Dennis' brother, who also served on the board, get a commitment from his church to raise the building funds for a church to be built on our campus. After concluding a successful trip to the States, I headed back home to Sudan.

When I got back home, we welcomed another member onto our Harvesters team by the name of Mourice (pronounced "Morris") Akuno. Before joining our team, Mourice, though originally from Kenya, attained his degree from a university in India and had been working as an administrator at a Christian school in Rwanda. God then called him to work in Sudan. That is when we were presented the opportunity to hire him as a teacher. After a short while, we recognized he had a superior intellect and leadership abilities, so we promoted him to be the administrator of Harvesters' Primary School.

Mr. Mourice Akuno

I am truly grateful the Lord has brought together individuals like Mr. Mourice (as we call him), Lance, Pastor Pooshani, and the list goes on to serve God at Harvesters by showing love and compassion to children and the community in need. It is a reminder to me of what God speaks of in Romans 12:4–8, "For as in one body we have many members, and the members do not all have the same function, so we, though many, are one body in Christ, and individually members one of another. Having gifts that differ according to the grace given to us, let us use them: if prophecy, in proportion to our faith; if service, in our serving; the one who teaches, in his teaching; the one who exhorts, in his exhortation; the one who contributes, in generosity; the one who leads, with zeal; the one who does acts of mercy, with cheerfulness" (ESV). To God be the glory!

Sixteen

Breaking Point
(2006)

On January 9, 2005, the Sudan People's Liberation Army (SPLA), the Sudanese People's Liberation Movement (SPLM), and the government of Sudan signed a peace agreement, ending the civil war that had been going on for decades between the northern and southern parts of Sudan. Sadly, Darfur, a region in western Sudan, was left out of the process, leaving tens of thousands of people to continue suffering from the bloodshed. Because Darfur is hundreds of miles from our campus, we were not directly affected by what was going on there. However, the Lord's Resistance Army (LRA), a rebel group out of Uganda led by Joseph Kony, did affect the security of our campus. The LRA was notorious for abducting children, taking young girls as sex slaves, and brainwashing young boys into killing people without cause.

By early 2006 we were warned that the LRA had crossed over into Sudan. At the time of the warning, one of the missionary nurses and I were the only expatriates on our campus. Dennis and Lance were back in the States, Mourice was on holiday in Uganda, and Pooshani was on holiday in Malaysia.

The nurse and I learned the rebel group had pillaged their way to the Congo where they established a base so they could terrorize more innocent people. Since the Congo–Sudan border is not all that far from our campus, the SPLA placed twelve extra soldiers to help safeguard us.

Early one evening a village boy came running down the road repeatedly yelling, "The LRA is here!" Upon hearing his frantic warning, everyone fled to the dorms, and the soldiers assumed their fighting positions. I immediately got on my satellite phone and called Bishop Elias, telling him what we had just heard. He informed me that many people were evacuating our area and coming into town because they heard the same thing. He then told me he was sending a couple of big trucks for us. He said for us to get all the children ready, start walking toward town, and they would pick us up. He would send out more soldiers to help protect us as well. By then it was dark, and I ran into the house with our oldest orphan, James Ladu. I began using my flashlight frantically trying to find my passport and money, my mind racing. Ladu, who could see I was fumbling around said, "Mama, just cool down."

After gathering my passport and the money we had on hand, we were told to leave and let the soldiers guard the campus. Hearing that made me heartsick. I wondered if there would be anything left as a result of an encounter with the LRA. I knew our possessions were just things, but they were all the children had ever had.

At that point the trucks were pulling onto our campus to pick us up. We, however, did not feel at peace about leaving, fearing that those children who could not get onto the trucks would have to walk, and they might get lost in the dark. When the trucks pulled up, several soldiers jumped off and walked over to where I was standing. One top security man then approached me and said, "It's your call, Mama. What do you want to do?"

When our nurse went inside to help the children get ready, what she saw was heart wrenching. Many of the children were trying to get all their belongings into their bed sheets, tied up, and ready to carry out. Several children were in the corners crying. Others were frantically looking for their siblings. She began to console them while I was outside trying to make a decision about whether to leave or stay. If we left I would have to choose who would go on the trucks and who had to walk. Several housemothers who were living with us and caring for the children were concerned for their children as well. They began to push their children toward the front so they could be the first to get on the trucks. Some of the teachers were saying, "Mama, please take my children too."

I felt so pressured, as though the entire world had been laid on my shoulders in that moment. In my state of panic, I failed to recall Jesus' words, "Take my yoke upon you . . . for my yoke is easy and my burden is light" (Matthew 11:29–30). Finally I came to a decision to stay. But some refused to go back inside, so we had to assure them it would be safer on campus than anywhere else. Their fears were grounded, and I understood why—the couple of years of peace in their lives seemed to be coming to an end.

I phoned Bishop Elias, thanked him, and said I was sending the trucks back without us. He told me to leave the kids there with the local staff, but we were to leave at once.

I protested, "No, I can't leave. I just can't do it. I won't even consider it!"

He replied, "Okay, but we will leave twenty-four soldiers with you for the night."

Not long after that the soldiers sent a couple of their men down the road to scout out where the LRA were. By that time many village people were coming to our campus, wanting to stay with us for safety. When the scouts returned they said the LRA were not as close as the boy had said. They were about five miles from us, which for me was too close for my comfort. While all that was taking place, I had been sending "telegram" prayers upward, and I knew others were praying as well.

Still afraid of the unknown, many of the children slept fully dressed with their backpacks on, thinking they might have to run in the night. Our nurse and I did not sleep at all. We made a pot of coffee and stayed up for the night, comforting the children and the housemothers, reminding them God was looking out for all of us.

The soldiers, however, took their positions ready to fight to protect us. I had never seen the soldiers act so seriously as they stood there alert and watching for any sign of the LRA approaching. But thankfully there were no signs that night. In fact, the night was quieter than any of us expected.

When morning came we looked at each other and broke down. The tears flowed steadily from our eyes, releasing all the tension and angst that had built up throughout the night. We had not fully realized what was happening to us until that very moment when we were able to relax and let go. Until that point we had to hold things together for the sake of the little ones. But I know it was truly God who enabled us.

After that initial night, it ended up taking several weeks before things were back to normal, if there is such a thing in Sudan.

Not long after the LRA scare, Dennis and Lance returned to the campus. While it seemed as though all my chaotic and trying experiences in Sudan happened while Dennis was away, we soon were about to face a Sudanese trial together.

One particular day, I was sitting under the mango tree at the orphanage with a friend, talking and playing with the little children. I glanced up toward where we held school, which was about a block from where we were sitting, and I noticed a man on the ground with a group of people around him. I recognized the man by his shirt. It was Dennis! I screamed for Lance to come out of his house, and we both started running over to the schoolyard where Dennis was.

As we approached I saw one of our older students who attended the secondary school on our campus was watching another student kick Dennis. When the boy kicking Dennis saw Lance and me coming, he started running for the gate where our guard was standing with his AK-47. As the guard opened the gate for him to pass through, the student grabbed the AK-47 from the guard. Afraid someone would be shot, I quickly yelled for the children to get inside the dining hall as the guard fought to get his gun back. That's when an older boy walking by the gate intervened, grabbing the student from behind so the guard could retrieve his gun. Boy, were we thankful that God had providentially sent that older boy to help!

Apparently those troubled students were some of the boys who had been expelled from our secondary school because they had been giving our teachers a hard time.

The boys decided to come back to the school with an attitude, threatening the teachers. Once Dennis was able to regroup, he explained he had gone over to see what was going on, and that's when one of the boys kicked him to the ground.

By that time we had been serving in Sudan for more than five years, teaching our orphans as well as many children from the surrounding villages. I was mortified to see the very boys we were trying to help attacking Dennis. It was alarming to say the least. In fact things got worse as those boys went into town to the education office, claiming Dennis had hit them. When we arrived with the teachers, Bishop Elias, and other witnesses, we explained our side. After much discussion the staff at the office believed us and called for the students to shake our hands and apologize. We learned after that experience that some of those students were in the SPLM, which explained why they were so forceful with Dennis. It was all they knew from being trained to fight for their freedom.

We then prayerfully thought about what had happened and determined it was in the best interest of the ministry to forego running a secondary school on our campus and focus instead on the primary school. Between having to make that decision and thinking about what Dennis had gone through (though he came through the incident without bodily injury), I felt defeated. For the first time since coming to Sudan, I wanted to pack up and leave. But Dennis and Lance helped me put the ordeal into a broader perspective. There was a deeper meaning to all of it, and we began to ponder how God must have felt when they betrayed and crucified His Son, Jesus Christ, and what Jesus Himself must have been feeling. We knew then that the Bible would show us how to respond.

After digging into Scripture, we determined that experience would not deter us in any way from the work we were called to do. The words of Abraham's servant say it best, "As for me, the LORD has led me" (Genesis 24:27). Moreover, who could choose to do otherwise than to continue in obedience when the Lord promises that in quietness and trust shall be our strength (see Isaiah 30:15)?

SEVENTEEN

I Surrender
(2006)

$\mathcal{O}$n June 5, 2006, I left for the States because my mother needed to have surgery. During one of her doctors' appointments that May, the doctors found some lumps they thought were hernias, but they were not certain and wanted to check it out. So they scheduled her surgery for late June. When I called her via my satellite phone to see how her appointment went, I could tell she sounded a bit concerned. I decided then, instead of waiting to show up by late June in time for the surgery, I should fly back to be with her as soon as possible. So I did.

Mother's surgery went well, and the lumps they discovered were indeed hernias. A few days after her surgery, I went to Walmart to pick up a few things. As I was shopping, my cell phone rang, so I answered. It was Shay calling to tell me that Pooshani had been trying to send me an email but was unable to send it. By that time Pooshani and I had grown close, and she knew with all that was going on with my mother I was not to be bothered about the everyday things back in Sudan. So when I heard from Shay that she was trying to reach me, I knew something was up.

Shay went on to tell me that Pooshani said Dennis wasn't feeling well. In fact, he was having pain in his chest and arm. That was all I needed to hear. I said, "Shay, we need to get him out of there. He is having a heart attack." She instructed me to go home and wait for a call, so I left my cart right in the middle of the store and ran to my car.

When I got in my car, I immediately phoned my oldest son, Corey. I began to cry as I told him his father was having a heart attack, and we needed to leave immediately for Kampala, Uganda. I went back to my apartment, mind racing, thinking *What should I do? If I leave now, he is going to pass me in the air.* So I called Bishop Elias and asked him to help me.

He said, "Just wait. I will try to have Dennis evacuated to Uganda."

So I did. I waited all night for his call, but nothing. The next day the phone rang, and it was Dennis. Yes, Dennis! He called using the satellite phone and told me what was happening. He said as long as he sat still and did not move, he was not in pain. I told him where he could find some nitroglycerin that was given to us to take to Sudan in case something like that ever happened. And I told him I would meet him in Kampala.

Just after we got off the phone, I heard from Bishop Elias. He said they could not get a plane to evacuate Dennis for about five days.

I said, "Elias, he will die if you don't get him out."

Praise God that Elias was able to make arrangements for Pooshani to fly with Dennis to Kampala a day and a half later. They kept him in the Kampala hospital for four days, but the only thing they could do was stabilize him so we could get him to the States.

While all that was going on, Corey was going to come with me to meet Dennis, but he did not have a passport, and there wasn't enough time to get one. To add to my anxiety, I had to wait a couple of days to find a flight that would coordinate with Dennis in Kampala. By the time I got there, Dennis had been discharged from the hospital and was waiting for me at a motel. He was weak and became short of breath with every step he took. We had to spend two more nights in the motel room waiting for a flight to open up so we could fly to the States. Our last night there, as I was sitting in a chair and Dennis was lying on the bed with a very serious look on his face, he said to me, "You must not move around on the bed."

I knew as I watched him spray the nitro under his tongue that he was having horrible chest pains. Morning finally arrived, and we left for the airport. At the airport, we waited in line, and when it was finally our turn, we were told we could not go because we did not have clearance to land and get off the plane in London.

I said, "What do you mean we don't have clearance?"

They said, "Your doctor ordered oxygen for the plane, but he didn't tell us how much to give you, so you can't go."

Outraged, I tried to tell them that the doctor had given Dennis permission to travel because there was nothing they could do for him in Africa, and if we didn't get him to the States he would die. But my pleas were not effective, and we were not allowed on that flight.

I sat Dennis in the cafeteria to wait while I went with an airport staff member to try and contact London and get approval for Dennis to land there. After several hours on the phone with London, it became apparent that the only way to get him out of there was not to acknowledge his medical condition. So we decided to bypass needing medical clearance by removing his name from the current record and starting a new one with no mention of his medical issue.

Finally we were able to get on the next flight, which was seven hours later than our original flight. That flight, however, was not direct to London. We had to first stop in Nairobi, Kenya, where we had another seven-hour layover. But believe me, we were never so happy to be on a flight than we were that day! While it seemed everything was working against us, we knew from our years of serving God that He was always faithful. He kept telling us through it all, *I will never leave you or forsake you,* and we knew He was right there with us. And were we going to need Him!

When we arrived in London, we found ourselves in the middle of a national terrorist situation. They announced over the airport intercom that all flights to the United States were canceled, and when we could get on a flight we would not be able to bring any carry-on bags. So we had to stand in a four-hour line to check our bags. Dennis remained calm throughout the whole ordeal, but I could see he was sweating. By then it had become something of a joke, a sick joke to be sure!

Exasperated, I threw up my arms, laughed, and said, "Hallelujah, Lord! Please take us home!" Dennis, sitting in a seat beside me, joined in the laughter.

Dennis, being the wonderful man he is and knowing my anxiety, calmed my fears in his own sweet way by holding hands with me. Our every thought was a prayer. We knew God is a prayer-hearing and prayer-answering God, and He was listening to our prayers.

After several more hours, we finally boarded the plane, only to sit for two-and-a-half hours on the tarmac. When we finally landed in Chicago, we were met by Dennis' brother, David Klepp, who drove us another four hours to a hospital in Green Bay, Wisconsin. The hospital admitted Dennis immediately. That next morning the surgeon did open-heart surgery on Dennis, performing five bypasses.

But our trial was not over just yet. Because Dennis had been put on blood thinners in Uganda, the surgeon and his team had a difficult time stopping the bleeding after the surgery. So Dennis ended up having to spend the next five days in the intensive care unit (ICU). Since his condition was so critical, and we did not know what the outcome would be, the whole family was there for their prayers and support. Corey spent the next several nights at my side in the ICU waiting room, waiting to hear his father's outcome.

My biggest fear at that time was wondering what I would do if Dennis died. While I felt okay focusing on comforting my family and them comforting me, that didn't keep me from worrying about Lance and the new family we had made in Sudan. In fact since I first got that call from Shay about Dennis, all kinds of anxious thoughts crossed my mind. I thought, *Surely this is not what God wants for me.* So I had to take myself in hand and, over and over again, turn myself and all my fears over to God, reflecting on His Word to not let my heart be troubled and to not be afraid (John 14:27). I asked God specifically to quiet my anxious fears, to give me peace in the midst of that personal storm, and to be with the surgeon and nurses who were His tools. Above all I asked God to be the Great Physician on behalf of my husband. However, I knew if anything did happen to Dennis, he would be safe in heaven with Jesus.

As I stayed in the Lord our Father's care, I was able to be and do for my husband and family members all that was needed. And while I definitely felt overwhelmed through it all, God was once again faithful. Dennis recovered quickly. In fact just three weeks after he had surgery, he was out golfing!

During that difficult time I struggled to see if God's will was for Dennis and me to suffer or for Him to heal Dennis. I now believe God wanted both because in my despair I was reminded that I can and need to put my trust in Him. In our situation Dennis received one of God's miracles through the use of modern medicine and the answering of prayers from hundreds of people asking the Lord to do that what was exceedingly good for Dennis and his family. And while I will never understand why all sick people are not healed, or why some suffer seemingly more than others, I do know one thing: His Word says, "We know that in all things God works for the good of those who love him, who have been called according to his purpose" (Romans 8:28).

Eighteen

Expansion
(2007–2008)

*A*fter Dennis' recovery we returned to Sudan to continue with the ministry and to see what God had in store for us next. Harvesters' orphanage and school in Yei, Sudan, had been up and running for six years by then. Our campus included dormitories for the boys and girls, showers and latrines, our house and staff housing, a dining hall, a clinic, a newly built church, and some school buildings, inclusive of a library, classrooms, and a school office. By the grace of God we were growing.

I knew, however, the need in the southern region of Sudan was great, and expansion into other areas was something the Lord lay on my heart to do. So Dennis and I spoke with Bishop Elias about some of the areas where we should consider building an orphanage and school. Once we weighed all of our options, we determined our next campus would be near the community of Terekeka, Sudan. Terekeka is located on the Nile River and is home to the Mundari tribe, which is comprised of cow herders. Our goal was to model the Terekeka campus after our campus in Yei, with an orphanage as well as a school and church that served the orphans and local community.

Interestingly, when Dennis and Bishop Elias went to Terekeka to meet with officials about building an orphanage and school there, the chief from the area told them that Muslims had just come a few days earlier to propose the same

Lance with Building Blocks

idea. The chief proceeded to tell Dennis and Bishop Elias that he told the Muslim men, "No thanks, we already have others coming to do this." But at that time the chief really did not know Dennis and Bishop Elias would arrive just a couple days later. That was further confirmation to us that Terekeka was the right place, because they wanted Christian missionaries to come there and build. It was ever so clear to me that God was at work and preparing the way.

By 2007 Lance and Dennis broke ground on the new Terekeka campus. They needed help, so they hired some local workers and also brought some of the men from Yei who had been with us for years. While Dennis and I were available to assist, ultimately Lance took on the responsibility for getting the Terekeka campus up and running.

Over the course of his first year living in Terekeka, I was privileged to observe Lance's dedication to serving God by serving those in need. He specifically did that by embracing the natives' way of life by living in a tent and washing, bathing, and drinking from the Nile. That was no easy adjustment, especially doing it alone. So Dennis and I started praying that God would bless Lance with a good wife to serve with him.

Lance Relaxing After a Hard Day

Nineteen

Cause for Celebration
(2008–2011)

In January 2008 our oldest and very helpful orphan, James Ladu, who was twenty-one years old at the time, traveled to Terekeka with a team from Harvesters to begin construction of our new orphanage. While James was there he started asking locals about his parents' whereabouts and if they were alive, but unfortunately no one knew anything. I could tell that though the work on the new orphanage was rewarding in many ways for James, he returned to Yei discouraged to have learned nothing about his family. But as God so often does, He showed us that He was not finished with James's story.

Not long after the team got back to Yei, an unexpected group of visitors arrived at the campus. It was James's parents, older brother, Abraham, and a younger brother he never knew he had, Pitia, who was then nine. Once James got word that his family was at the campus, he became nervous and began to cry. It was the first time I had ever seen James cry. Their extraordinary family reunion was something spectacular to see! As it turned out, James's family had also spent all of those years not knowing what happened to their son during the war. As overwhelming and indescribable as this moment was, it was truly a miracle. Perhaps James's words say it best:

> I was happy and shocked at the same time. I thought I would never see my parents again. If it were not for Harvesters, I would not have any

education, healthcare, and feeding. They have helped me in every area. Spiritually I have grown to know Christ as my Savior. There is no one else like Harvesters in southern Sudan helping us. Thank you to our donors!

James Ladu's Family Reunion

While there are definitely times when change seems impossible, I know every time someone comes to help or makes a donation, a seed of hope is planted in the children's lives because they have been remembered. As more people continue to help, more hope rises, and eventually change we felt impossible begins to occur.

Not long after James's miraculous family reunion, a medical team through Youth with a Mission (YWAM) came to serve at our campus. On the team was a Christian nurse by the name of Kim. During Kim's trip she and Lance met, and a relationship blossomed. A year later, on September 13, 2009, they got married. Dennis and I were thrilled to have our prayers answered. But most of all we rejoiced and praised God for the wonderful way He orchestrates our lives.

After the wedding Lance and Kim spent a few months back in the States before returning to Terekeka, Sudan, to start the orphanage and school. Dennis, Caleb, and I, however, headed back to Sudan to continue the process of making Caleb an official part of our family. On December 3, 2009, we were given the official adoption certificate for Caleb, naming Dennis and me his parents! Because the criteria for adopting a Sudanese child required one to live in Sudan for three years or more, we knew we were one of the few who was ever approved for adoption in Sudan. We knew our adoption of Caleb in Sudan was a crucial step in applying for adoption of him in the States and his dual citizenship. Needless to say we were grateful we had gotten the Sudanese adoption completed so we could begin to work on the process of adopting him in the States as well.

Mama Lilly, Caleb, and Dennis with Caleb's Sudanese Adoption Certificate

By summer 2010 Lance and Kim officially opened the Terekeka orphanage with twenty-seven orphans on their roster. In Yei we had grown to more than one hundred and fifty orphans on our campus. And while the mango trees had provided us almost nine years of shade for our school teachings and chapel services in Yei, we were excited to finally have a school built for the five hundred students attending at that time. Our church building, too, was a cause for celebration, as it had been built and served the local community since 2008.

Harvesters' Assembly Church

With all the growth we were experiencing, I still recognized there was another issue in the community that needed to be addressed. Because there is not adequate medical care in Sudan, the mortality rate is one of the highest in the world. It's astonishing to think, but statistics show that one in five children will die before the age of five, and one in ten women will die during childbirth in Sudan. Based on these facts alone, my heart became burdened to do something. So I started the conversation with our board about what could be done.

After much prayer and deliberation, the board and Dennis and I felt we should build a hospital and have missionary doctors come to run it on a long-term basis. We had come to the conclusion that with a hospital we could be much more effective serving the community than was possible with the small clinic on our campus. More specifically we decided the hospital would serve women and children with the goal of reducing illness and death from preventable and treatable diseases, as well as improving pregnancy outcomes by providing care

84

before, during, and after pregnancy. With plans in place and partial funds raised, we started construction of the hospital in 2011.

On July 3, 2011, a long-awaited dream for the people of the southern Sudan region became a reality. The new nation of South Sudan was born! I remember being on our campus in Yei at the time, hearing the news as it spread from person to person: "South Sudan is free!" As the housemothers and workers on our campus got the word, we all gathered in celebration and started dancing in jubilee for the occasion. It was a remarkable day for me to get to experience alongside my Sudanese family.

Later that same year we flew home to make our adoption of Caleb official in the States. We also had him naturalized as a U.S. citizen so he has dual citizenship. As things came to a close with Caleb's adoption, I was able to reflect on the journey we had been on to that point. While it took almost ten years to make him an official part of our family, I reminded myself that it took decades for South Sudan to win its independence from the North. It was evident to me then that God always meets the needs of His people in His perfect timing. And I can say that in that year alone, in His perfect timing, we had a lot to look forward to and celebrate.

South Sudan Flag

Twenty

Going Strong
(2012–2013)

March 2012 brought about even more cause for celebration. Lance and Kim welcomed their first baby, a boy named Gideon, into the world. His House of Hope Hospital officially opened in Yei and ground was broken in Terekeka for a school to be built. Not only that, we made plans to build a vocational school in Yei called The Joshua and Esther Center, named after two people in the Bible who showed great faith, perseverance, and quiet courage. We believe this center will develop our boys and girls into a skilled, entrepreneurial Christian workforce who desires to contribute to South Sudan's promising future.

HOSPITAL

With the opening of the hospital we brought on board two long-term missionary doctors and two missionary nurses. I must say, it's been an awesome thing to witness the impact that our long-term medical team and visiting medical teams have had on the community. Their heart to serve has made such a difference in the lives of the Sudanese people—so much so, that some of our orphans have been inspired to become nurses and doctors themselves one day.

And while it is amazing to see what can be accomplished by having a hospital on campus, it is important to note that God is not limited by our limitations.

Lance, Kim, and Gideon Klepp

His House of Hope Hospital and Staff

Christopher Mungu, who contracted meningitis back in 2006, is a prime example of that. Fully recovered, Christopher is now twenty years old, married, and has a child of his own. In 2012 he visited our campus to thank us for the role we played in his life. And I'll say, it never gets old hearing how well our kids are doing.

CHURCH

With a heart to serve, Pastor Pooshani helped establish and lead Harvesters Assembly Church at our campus in Yei. She also spearheaded our discipleship program by teaching the older children to take responsibility for conducting Bible study groups, translating the sermons from Juba Arabic to English, teaching Sunday school, and participating in other outreach activities. Older children are now going out to the villages and teaching the Word of God in home community groups. I have seen many people come to Christ through these efforts, setting them free from oppression in Sudan. It is even more evident to me now that these children will become great godly leaders for South Sudan.

Harvesters' Assembly Church Leaders

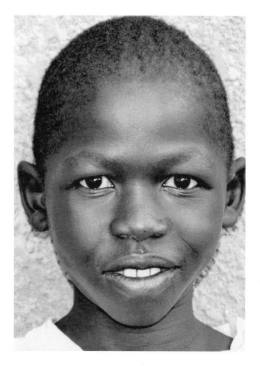

Obediah Dennis

Our older boys have started meeting together on Saturday nights to pray and worship the Lord. They've been doing it on their own; no one is telling them to. It's been a beautiful sight to see God using these children in so many ways—from the youngest to the oldest. In fact, the boys' Saturday night prayer time has now grown into a community-wide prayer time on Saturday evenings in our church. All of our children are learning the importance of the power of prayer. This was evident in our orphan Obediah's story, when I witnessed children as young as three laying their hands on him and praying. Their prayers were answered, and now Obediah is a healthy young boy who enjoys playing with the toy tin cars he has learned to make for the younger boys. His infectious smile reminds me daily of the Lord's power to heal. To God be the Glory!

During the summer of 2013 my dear sister Pooshani completed her ten years of service with us. She accomplished so much! One of her greatest legacies is her mentoring to Hillary, a local Sudanese man, who is now being trained to be our church's pastor. Pooshani also helped to train an American couple, Doug and Denise Burrows, to come oversee the church and children's ministry alongside Brother Hillary. Denise Burrows is Dennis' sister. And while I'll miss serving alongside Pooshani, we are so grateful to have Doug and Denise on our team!

ORPHANAGE AND SCHOOL

Together, both campuses in Yei and Terekeka care for almost two hundred orphans and provide schooling for more than five hundred students. In 2012 our primary school in Yei boasted a top-scoring student in all of South Sudan. But more important than that, we have seen doors opened for these children through the additional education they're now getting. To ensure our kids have an opportunity for further education beyond our primary school, we have started a scholarship program called the Hannah Scholarship Fund, designed to pay for secondary (high) school for deserving students, and support further education for children interested in going on to training school or university once they have completed primary and secondary school.

Harvesters' Primary School on the Yei Campus

James Ladu, for instance, who came to us at age fourteen in 2001, has since graduated from university in Juba with a degree in business and has aspirations to work in the government. For me, it's stories like James's that reaffirm why God has called Harvesters to South Sudan. By providing care and education for these children, they have the opportunity to flourish in their community and live as the Lord wills them to.

Terekeka Primary School Classroom

STAFF

As of the writing of this book, we employ more than one hundred locals on our campuses. In fact, Mama Itiya, our first widow and housemother, is still with us to this day. She works hard taking care of the orphans and her family. We are so very grateful to have seen her love of God develop and grow into what it is today.

Mr. Mourice's continuous hard work has earned him the position of campus administrator, which oversees our entire work in Yei, including the orphanage, school, church, and hospital. He has demonstrated, through his time with Harvesters, an understanding of cultural relations that has proven to be invaluable to us expatriates. This is why it comes as no surprise to me that he has long had a desire to become a diplomat. Here are some of his words:

> To make a long story short, it seems that God plans for me to be the
> diplomat I had always wanted to become. This became a reality when

Mama Lilly welcomed me into the Harvesters' orphanage. I ended up in a place where there is a need to show orphans who have experienced hopelessness how to become better human beings, while treating them with a kind heart.

Personal

While my father has since passed and my mother continues to struggle with her health, I know both of them know Jesus Christ as their Savior, and that is a comfort to me to know we will be reunited with one another in heaven.

In 2013 Dennis had a tumor surface under his eye and had to return home for treatment. We pray faithfully God will continue to heal him. He still goes strong though, working hard on converting the old pyatt (cafeteria hut) into a computer lab for our vocational school and overseeing the expansion of our hospital. I am so grateful to be married to him. He has faithfully served God by my side, and I feel blessed every day to have him in my life.

Corey and Jodi Klepp's Family

My son, Corey, and his wife, Jodi, and their sons, Tristan and Santana, and daughter, Faith, and her husband, Ian Answorth, live in Jackson, Wisconsin. They, too, have their own ministry working with underprivileged children. I couldn't be happier to see the impact they're having on the youth in their community.

Lance and Kim continue to lead our campus in Terekeka with more than forty-five orphans. It has been great to see how far that campus has come. In 2013 they finished construction of some of the classrooms for the primary school. Not only is it amazing to reflect on what God has done in Terekeka, it's also been a blessing to see that Lance has surprised himself by preaching God's Word throughout his time on the mission field. This is a further reminder that with God anything is possible.

As for Caleb, he is growing up! He often travels back with me when I head to the States for fundraising and speaking engagements. On these trips he has had the opportunity to learn martial arts, and to experience playing in snow during Wisconsin winters as well as going to water parks in the summer. Dennis and I feel so blessed to be able to call Caleb one of our sons. God had shown me that even though we didn't have an orphanage built at the time we took Caleb in, through His provision, we could care for Caleb as He intended.

TWENTY-ONE

Our Story Continues
(2013–2014)

*I*n May 2013 Dennis and I came back to the States for one of Harvesters' board meetings. After the meeting ended the plan was for Dennis to head back to South Sudan, and Caleb and I would stay and care for my ailing mother. I began to struggle about how long I should stay with my mother, given her state of health. On one hand I felt I couldn't leave for South Sudan because I had a gut feeling it might be my mom's last year, and I wanted to be there for her. On the other hand, I knew there were things I needed to be handling in Sudan. I really felt torn, so I prayed. God answered by giving me a peace about staying with my mom, so I did and continued to direct things from the States regarding the ministry.

By late July it was announced that South Sudan President Salva Kiir Mayardit of the Dinka tribe fired Vice President Riek Machar of the Nuer tribe, as well as most of his cabinet. President Kiir proceeded to install a skeleton cabinet until future elections could be held. However, despite President Kiir's attempt to clean house, it aroused a familiar fear in the people of South Sudan—a fear of what has been prevalent their entire lives, the reality that another civil war would likely ensue.

When December 2013 came so did reports of violent attacks within the nation's capital, Juba. It was thought that former Vice President Machar rallied Neur soldiers in a coup attempt to overtake the capital. Though Machar denied the attempt, the situation, coupled with the overwhelming economic hardships already in place across the country, resulted in unrest across multiple regions in South Sudan. And while our campuses in both Yei and Terekeka were safe to that point, the violence reached nearby areas that caused those there to take precautionary measures.

It was so sad! This time it was not the North against the South; it was tribes within South Sudan fighting each other. That political and tribal struggle broke my heart as I learned of the atrocities that took place. Children ran into the bush to hide, going without food and water and seeing their parents killed right in front of them. Tens of thousands of people had to leave their homes and flee to the bush or neighboring countries.

Given these recent events, God rekindled the familiar feeling within me of longing to be in South Sudan with Dennis, helping my Sudanese family: the widows, orphans, teachers, and others I've lived with over the past thirteen years. And even though I wasn't able to be there since the violence broke out, I was encouraged to hear that the older kids really stepped up and helped in all areas of the campus. It is refreshing to know those we care for are truly family for one another, and I couldn't be prouder of that!

As South Sudan struggles to build a new nation at this writing, I am reminded and encouraged that Harvesters, no matter the circumstances, continues to be blessed. I believe a large part of God's hand of blessing being upon us has to do with our commitment to stay in the midst of war. We have followed God's direction by sticking it out and living with the local Sudanese people through their hardships and trials, and during that time we gradually won their respect and friendship. Now we are accepted as a valuable part of the community.

I truly believe God has and will continue to protect the hope that dwells in the hearts of His people. Hope for restoration. It's important to say we mustn't ever give up hope and faith that God is doing something greater than we could ever envision. And regardless of how the political state of the nation turns out, those we care for will continue to need to be fed and provided for as long as the

Lord calls on us to do so. It is my humble request that you please pray for this new nation and its future and most importantly the people who call it home.

Our plans for the future, with Harvesters' basic model in place, are to duplicate its success in several other regions of South Sudan. God's vision is ever growing and expanding as we submit ourselves to His will. He has taught us to live and work within the Sudanese culture, not to impose our culture on theirs. We have learned to live the life of Christ as examples and share with our Sudanese neighbors and friends the Word of God, allowing the Holy Spirit to change their hearts and lives.

As I reflect on our time in South Sudan, I can see that God has taught me so many amazing things, especially how to trust Him. Who would have ever thought Harvesters would be what it is today? It's funny to think how in the past I thought about our limitations and how we couldn't accomplish what has been achieved, but God is limitless. He has taught me not to plan around what I think Harvesters can afford, but rather around what He has put in my heart, and to let Him provide for it. It is true that He who calls us will equip us. In fact, if our vision is small enough that we can provide for it, it probably is not God's vision. And I know I would not want any other life than the one to which God has called me.

I want the body of Christ to know we could not have done this without the continual prayers, gifts, help, and love of God's people. This ministry is not about Dennis and me. It is about the entire body of Christ working together to give help and hope to people who are in such a sad and difficult place. And in doing so we show them the Father-heart of God and His Son Jesus, and further the kingdom of God for His glory. This is God's mission. It is His vision and dream. We are simply His servants, carrying out His will.

Stories of Hope

The following stories are about just a few of the many orphans for whom Harvesters has been fortunate to care. While these stories fall short of conveying the needs of the children entirely, they do help paint a picture of the fallout of a war-torn region and its ongoing struggles. These stories also help demonstrate the hope that is in Christ and the hope that is in following in obedience the Lord's will for our lives.

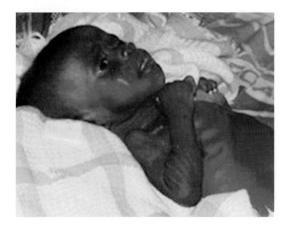

Nyoko on Arrival at Harvesters

NYOKO JOSEPH LASU
(2008–PRESENT)

One day shortly after noon, a lady came to our His Merciful Hands Clinic with a tiny baby. The lady had come to get milk for the child from our formula feeding program. Fortunately we had a visiting medical team from San Francisco there, and they were able to evaluate and set up care for the child. It turned out Nyoko, as we call him, was three months old and only weighed six pounds! Nyoko had apparently stopped eating, had severe diarrhea, and was the most severely dehydrated child we had ever seen, which says something. Nyoko was so dehydrated that the only way to administer nutrition was through an IV. After also learning that his mother was severely disabled and that his father, who was rather elderly, had a relative who was caring for him back in the village, we knew we had to save this child! I praised God that the medical team was there and had the equipment necessary to save him.

Nyoko Lasu Today

Nyoko required round-the-clock care for many days. With a washbasin for a crib, a homemade blanket, a cap to keep his head warm, and tiny socks, we were able to fashion a small neonatal-type nursery in our one guest room on campus. Beds were made for the rotation of nurses who would be required to care for this small child of God.

Nyoko proved to be quite a fighter! After days on a feeding tube, Nyoko finally progressed to a bottle. Days later he weighed in at seven-and-a-half pounds and was gaining.

Situations like these have proven to me time and time again that God is not far off; He is ever near and a very present help in time of need. Nyoko would not have survived without the prayers and assistance of the visiting medical team.

Because his family was unable to care for him, Nyoko was welcomed full-time at our orphanage. We all agreed on his name, Nyoko Joseph Miller-Brown Lasu! While it was a big title for such a little guy, it suited him. The significance behind his middle names is that they are a combination of the names of those who helped to save his life—Joseph for the pediatrician with the medical team, missionary nurses Miller and Brown, who rotated shifts caring for Nyoko during his recovery. It was the teamwork of the Lord and His people who pulled Nyoko through, so we thought we would give him a team name. Today little Nyoko is five years old and is in preschool. He loves to sit on the laps of our staff members and older children and is truly a bright spot in South Sudan!

SIKILI ABRAHAM (2009–PRESENT)

Matthew 24 talks about wars and rumors of wars and how evil will increase in the end times. It talks also about the importance of consistently living God's way and taking care of His people. Sudan has suffered from war for many years. I have personally seen the effects of the atrocities of this war. One was a little baby girl named Sikili Abraham. Sikili was just four months old when the LRA came into her village, killed her mother, and set their *tukul* (hut) on fire.

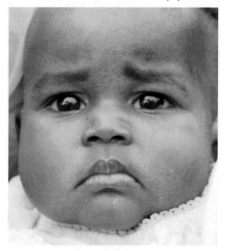

During that attack Sikili's father, Abraham, grabbed his infant daughter and two of his other children and fled on foot. They walked for many miles until a large vehicle picked them up.

While they were being driven to safety, the LRA appeared and began opening fire on the vehicle, killing

Sikili Abraham after Arrival

the driver. Abraham jumped out of the vehicle, dropping Sikili, and then fell on top of her, injuring her chest cavity. He and Sikili were later brought to the local hospital in Yei. She was not only injured in the chest, she was also severely dehydrated and required an IV in her head.

After Abraham recovered from his initial injuries, he brought Sikili to us. It was devastating to see how traumatized Abraham was after having lost his wife, home, and was left with an infant and two children. It was evident that caring for Sikili was too much for him. Before Abraham left us to care for Sikili, he took her hand and spoke to her. Though I did not understand what he said, I looked at Sikili, and my eyes filled with tears as I thought of what her father was going through. Abraham and Sikili's story is why we are here—to care for His people.

Sikili 2012

While Sikili came to us in a very fragile state, and her health seemed to improve under our care, we soon became challenged with her inability to move her legs, consistent crying, and persistent fever. In an effort to get the medical attention she needed, I sent her with one of our employees, Jacquee, to Uganda where she could get the evaluation and treatment she needed, not yet available in Yei.

On their journey to Uganda, Jacquee and Sikili were detained in an airport jail. The police were accusing Jacquee of stealing Sikili. Fortunately, after they called our campus in Yei to verify Jacquee's story, they released them both and gave them a police escort to the hospital!

It turned out that Sikili had septic arthritis in her hip, likely due to the trauma she suffered when she was dropped as her father was trying to escape from the LRA attack. Thankfully the doctor was able to perform surgery and drained the infection from her hip. Sikili has since recovered fully and is flourishing alongside the other children at the campus. It is my hope that one day she and Abraham, along with her two siblings, will reunite.

MILTON JUMA (2011–PRESENT)

On the afternoon of January 12, 2011, the fourth day of referendum voting when registered voters in Sudan voted for unity or secession from the North, ten-year-old Milton Juma fell from a mango tree. A branch broke beneath him, and he fell more than thirty feet, landing squarely on his face and chest. Because it was dry season, the ground was especially hard. Immediately, Milton's face began to swell and sweat covered his body as blood flowed from his ears, nose, and mouth.

One of our teenage boys helped carry Milton to our Harvesters Clinic. Unfortunately, there wasn't much our nurse at the clinic could do for him, considering the potential severity of his injuries. We knew Milton would need a thorough exam to ensure he was being treated properly. So Mr. Mourice quickly put Milton into the back of a Land Cruiser and drove to the nearest doctor while the rest of the adults gathered on Pastor Pooshani's porch to pray and discuss options.

It became apparent to us that because of the referendum voting going on, all the doctors had left the region. *All* of them.

Eventually, though, Mr. Mourice got Milton checked in to a local clinic. But there were no doctors there either, and the clinical officer was drunk. We decided to keep Milton at the clinic overnight in hopes of getting x-rayed in the morning. Amazingly Milton remained conscious and even asked for food during that time. While he did have back pain and bleeding continued, the swelling slowly subsided. That's when Milton, in his hospital bed, raised his hands in the air and cried out to God saying, "God, You are my only healer; please help me."

The patients nearby happened to witness Milton cry out to God and began to gather around him, amazed that this young boy who had suffered such a bad accident was crying out to God and in faith asking for healing. What a testimony!

The next morning Milton was discharged from the clinic and came back to Harvesters. It was touching to watch his older brother, Alex, come up to Milton, shed tears, kneel before him, and praise God for healing his brother.

Milton Juma Miraculously Healed

Because Milton's fall was so great, it was decided he should go to the International Hospital Kampala in Uganda for treatment. Ten days after the fall from the tree, Milton returned to Harvesters and was given a warm welcome from all the kids. Today Milton is back to his old self. He's smiling, laughing, and joking, and we are all so grateful for his amazing recovery and for all the provisions God gave us. We know God is the great Healer, and our prayer for Milton is that this experience will grow him in love, faith, and trust and that he will be a fervent servant of the Lord.

ELIZABETH PITA (2011–PRESENT)

In 2011 a small group of visiting partners went to visit the local hospital to watch some of our older orphans perform for the hospital staff and patients as part of our drama ministry program. After their drama was over, the group went to the children's ward to pray for the patients.

In going through the ward, they came across a young girl, Elizabeth, in very dire circumstances; she was terribly malnourished. At two years old she weighed less than fifteen pounds and could barely sit up from lack of energy. Her grandfather, who was there with her, asked if Harvesters could help. We learned that Elizabeth was from a village about five miles away. Her mother has epilepsy and had been unable to care for her daughter since her birth. The grandfather explained that those back in the village were troubled by his daughter's bizarre behavior (which was a symptom of her epilepsy). He went on to say that due to his daughter's illness she wasn't capable of caring for her daughter Elizabeth. She could hardly take care of herself. This had resulted in his trying to care for and protect little Elizabeth since she had been born. We knew he was doing

Elizabeth Pita at Arrival

the absolute best he could, given the situation, but it was not enough to sustain her.

So what were we to do? We're an orphanage after all, but over the years we have learned that we cannot take in every child. A child like Elizabeth would need one-on-one care for several months. Taking her in at that time would mean we would have to hire a new housemother to care for her. We also knew from many previous experiences this child deserved a chance to survive, to be loved and cared for, so we embraced Elizabeth and made her one of Harvesters' own. She was then blessed with one hundred fifty brothers and sisters!

Sadly Elizabeth's story is not unique to the children of South Sudan. But we do see, time and time again, how a good home, nutritious food, and loving care can literally bring the light back into children's eyes and give them hope and a chance at a good life, one where they will know their Savior, Jesus Christ.

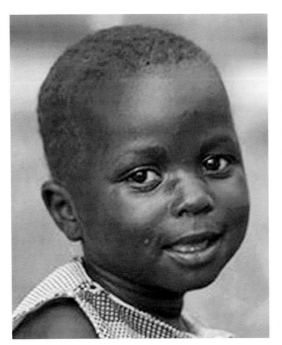

Elizabeth Pita Today

Now Elizabeth is four years old and is growing strong, healthy, and is as talkative and playful as she can be. We are truly grateful for God's grace and give Him the glory for being able to care for the orphans He brings to us in South Sudan.

To read more Harvesters' stories of Sudanese children in South Sudan, visit www. HRTN.org/media/#stories.

About the Author
Lillian Klepp and Harvesters Reaching the Nations

Lillian Klepp, wife of Dennis Klepp and cofounder of Harvesters Reaching the Nations, is a missionary serving in South Sudan, one of this world's most difficult and challenging countries. A native of Wisconsin, Lillian spent her professional career working as an occupational therapy assistant. Over many years she served in numerous roles in her church, including the roles of children's pastor and worship leader.

In 1999 Lillian was called by God to step out in faith and do even more. She and her husband, Dennis, a local building contractor, prayed for many months to discern the Lord's will for their future work. God spoke to their hearts, telling them to sell everything they had and go serve in Sudan. In 2001 they formed Harvesters Reaching the Nations, a nonprofit, nondenominational, Christ-centered organization committed to providing discipleship, education, and healthcare to orphans, as well as to vulnerable women and children in remote regions of the world. They sold their belongings and moved to Sudan, just the two of them, with $20,000 in savings and faith that this was God's will for them.

Known as "Mama Lilly" in South Sudan, she and Dennis now serve alongside ten other expatriate missionaries. They have more than one hundred local employees in two locations where they are caring for nearly two hundred orphans, more than five hundred school children, thousands of women and children through their hospital, and hundreds more through their local church.

HARVESTERS REACHING THE NATIONS

Will You Join Us?

We are working to realize a vision: a world where children are free from spiritual, economic and social poverty so they can better serve their communities as disciples of Christ.

For more information visit us online at HRTN.org or call us toll-free 877-867-7426.

Changing Lives...Bringing Hope.

Harvesters Reaching the Nations is a Christ-centered organization providing discipleship, education and health care to orphans as well as vulnerable women and children in remote regions of the world.

To sponsor a child(ren) at one of our campuses in South Sudan please visit our website: HRTN.org.